BEST BOSS
EVER

A Quick How-to-Guide for Inspiring Excellence as a Frontline Leader

by
Glenn Dorey

 FriesenPress

One Printers Way
Altona, MB R0G 0B0
Canada

www.friesenpress.com

ISBN
978-1-03-919185-3 (Hardcover)
978-1-03-919184-6 (Paperback)
978-1-03-919186-0 (eBook)

1. BUSINESS & ECONOMICS, LEADERSHIP

Distributed to the trade by The Ingram Book Company

This book is dedicated to my always supportive, generous, fun-loving awesome human being and big brother Peter Dorey (1959–2022) who never stopped asking when I was going to finish this book. I finally finished it, Peter!

Table of Contents

Introduction

I am writing this book for those bold enough to step into leadership roles for the first time and for those determined and dedicated enough to see leadership as a life-long vocation. I am also hopeful that this advice for leaders will make for a more rewarding, enjoyable and successful worklife for employees at the receiving end of good or bad frontline leadership.

My primary qualification for writing this book is that I have worked in leadership coaching and development in the industrial world (think smokestacks) for the past nineteen years. In addition to formal education (Bachelor and Master of Business Administration), I have been a corporate trainer, frontline leader, manager, and company executive. I have also been certified in various leadership modalities, such as Situational Leadership and Insights, and Emotional Intelligence.

The best education I have received by far, however, is from workers and leaders in the real world facing real challenges, inspiring their colleagues and teams to achieve great things. I mention workers because those being led are the ultimate judges of leadership competence.

Before writing this book, I interviewed ten experienced leaders whom I respect from a wide array of fields. Their views on the best frontline leadership were in alignment with what I have witnessed over the years. According to the group of leaders interviewed, there was considerable overlap on what makes a great frontline leader, and this also echoed my beliefs. The major themes described in this book will highlight this wisdom drawn from the real world. My best mentor on all matters to do with leadership is my brother Brian Dorey who took a chance on me, took me under his wing, and shared his wisdom and vision. Many of the concepts herein have roots linking to Brian.

I see being the *Best Boss Ever* for any individual as a realistic goal, primarily because the bar is not terribly high in many, even good, organizations. Being the best among a string of disappointing leaders is therefore not difficult. Being a great boss will require hard work and commitment, however. It is doable and if you chose to make that your goal, you will become many people's "best boss ever."

The underlying challenge for any leader is to optimize the potential of their team. Everything in this book relates to a leader's ability to inspire great performance for those who they have the privilege to lead. It is not about a leader's own accomplishments, abilities, skills, and knowledge, but rather how they propel those around them to new heights. Just as proud parents see their children supersede their own performance, leaders should aim to develop their team members into far better employees and leaders than themselves.

Developing others and creating team momentum may seem straight-forward, but nothing could be further from the truth. It takes belief in yourself, continuous effort, and supreme tact to become an amazing leader. In fact, one of the things that holds many leaders back is a fear of failure to have the right presence, do the best things, and give the best advice in the right manner. It, along with everyday distractions and busyness, can lead to hesitancy that will certainly stand in the way of progress.

One obstacle for any budding leader is that many organizations value short-run results over long-term value. This makes it even more difficult to optimize long-term leader and team success. In many organizations where the focus is on short-term results, frontline leaders are encouraged to be intimately involved in every little detail to ensure zero mistakes and that today's results are acceptable. This approach leads to micromanagement, turns off the rest of the team, and creates medium and long-term underperformance. Even with this understanding, too many companies continue to choose short-term results and don't look past the present financial quarter.

Shareholders in publicly traded organizations are often very support-ive of the short-term results at any cost approach. Leaders (including those on the frontline) need to be cognizant of that background dynamic and realize that nobody has a greater interest in long-term success than they themselves. As great leaders gain more confidence, they will push back on organizational pressures when short-term decisions or direction threaten long-term viability or team success. This book will guide readers to take a longer-term view, value and respect people and reap the reward of optimized long-term commitment and results.

True leadership is not a title. Everybody can and should lead when their experience, skills, and perspective can advance a cause. I have learned much from my own mistakes and from a multitude of leaders at all levels of corporations in many sectors. One primary lesson is that one of a leader's most important roles is knowing when to get out of the way of competent, brilliant, and hard-working people. This requires humility, something lacking in any leader who believes their job is to always be right and always maintain control.

The motivation, dedication, and commitment of the people impacted by leadership behaviours is the real test of leadership effectiveness. If you want to determine how well a leader is performing, don't ask them, ask the people they lead. Colleagues and I have asked thousands of employees, supervisors, and managers what makes a great boss and what makes a bad one. These themes are woven into this book.

As a leader, you must realize that your team makes you successful. In order for this to happen, making them successful has to take precedent over making yourself shine. Anything you do to unleash their talents and efforts is reflected in your success. Therefore, your focus should be on them, not on you. Your job as a lone wolf, individual contributor, subject matter expert, or know-it-all is over. You may have been hired or promoted because of your technical knowledge and experience but leaning too heavily on your past knowledge and behaviours will lead to a stunted leadership journey. You must switch gears and think about how to support others in coming up with answers and making decisions.

Your direct reports need the same feeling of elation and satisfaction you got when saving the day at your last position, so don't steal their glory. This is something that I have been attempting to undo in leaders throughout my coaching career. In spite of an abundance of guidance, literature, and training, micromanagement is alive and well in modern work cultures. In fact, it is just as prevalent today as when I entered the work world thirty years ago. People who get their role as leader right are far less stressed, busy, overloaded, and burned-out, and they have successful, motivated teams. They also tend to have a more balanced life and a lot of good things happening beyond work.

If you want success, I encourage you to overcome the natural urge to be the centre of attention. Set aside whatever ego you have and be willing to help your team members shine. This will unleash breakthrough results because the synergy in a high-functioning team is always more powerful than a bunch of solo, heroic pursuits, especially from the leader.

In addition, great teams also make attractive workplaces, with reduced stress, increased engagement, higher job satisfaction, and more likelihood for individual success. All of these factors play into competitiveness, employee attraction, and higher retention levels. People don't leave winning teams as often. If organizations want to attract the best and brightest talent, frontline leaders need to build teams that value people, ideas, and most of all, teamwork.

I have seen too many people land leadership jobs because of impressive individual contributions, without a speck of evidence that they can inspire a team. If you are saying, "That's me, though," don't worry; it's not complicated. This book will be refreshing for you because I will be asking you to back off and help others flourish. How hard is that? It's easy. The biggest issue may be staring back at you from the mirror!

If you are a woman reading this book, there has never been a better time to be entering the leadership realm. Women have long been underrepresented in management ranks, and the world is missing out. Organizations are beginning to realize that not only are they overlooking half of the population for leadership roles, but they are also missing tremendous leadership strengths that are typically more developed in women than men. Qualities such as higher empathy, better listening skills, and more willingness to collaborate are some examples. Of course, not all women have superior people leadership skills, but some notable differences in leader aptitude have been identified. In particular, the combination of both intellectual and emotional qualities, both critical to leadership, tend to be more common in women.[1]

The reason that this book is geared toward frontline leaders and not just leaders in general is that leading on the frontline is the hardest, most critical leadership job of all, and yet much of the literature on leadership is aimed at C-suite executives. Much of the advice is similar for frontline leaders because leadership at any level is about inspiring people to achieve great feats. Where frontline leadership differentiates from C-suite leadership is that frontline leaders live at the critical interface between worker and management roles. Leading at this level requires incredible tact and people skills to accomplish the real work of the organization while avoiding the us versus them culture that is far too prevalent. Without stellar frontline leadership, organizations fail to deliver up to potential, work culture is abysmal, discretionary effort is minimal, and turnover is inevitable. Organizational results are highly dependent on the skills, motivation, and inspirational abilities of frontline leaders, and they deserve every bit of support, encouragement, and professional growth possible.

In order to be the best boss ever, you will need to establish strong personal connection with everybody on your team and also any key person or people influencing your team. In order to do this, please realize the difference between online and in-person presence. This modern world, not to mention the worldwide pandemic we have all endured, has driven online communication to new heights. This is very efficient, green, and allows a much greater work life balance for many. It also fails to live up to the tremendous impact of in person meetings, observations, body language cues, ad hoc conversations, synergy, and general richness that only happens face to face. If you believe in building a team, truly connecting with people, and establishing relationships that will elevate commitment and performance, consider favouring in-person time over online time where possible. I fully realize this involves

---

1   Tony Schwartz, "What Women Know about Leadership that Men Don't," *Harvard Business Review*, October 30, 2012, https://hbr.org/2012/10/what-women-know-that-men-dont.

inconvenience and more time away from family and for some this may not be realistic. If you do have that luxury, in-person communication is just more impactful.

Conviction

CHAPTER 1
Vision

Great leaders see a better future. They understand the present and realize the challenges standing in the way. They see obstacles as surmountable and believe in others to make it happen. In fact, they depend on others rising to the challenge, working as a team to achieve every milestone. They see eye to eye with those facing challenges and they are there to help, support, and coach. They are convinced that the vision of the future is achievable and worthwhile, and their confidence rubs off on those around them.

Aim high! Nobody will be inspired by a vision or goal that strives to just be acceptable. At the start of his career Tiger Woods boldly aimed to surpass Jack Nicklaus's eighteen majors.[2] He didn't just aim to play and win on the PGA tour.

Some people believe that vision is exclusively the responsibility of high-ranking executives and not a priority for frontline supervisors and employees. This viewpoint is both arrogant and faulty. It is as if executives can command the future and rely on the cooperation and compliance of their employees to execute whatever dream or delusion they have. Executives would be wise to do everything in their power to understand the motivators for employees, frontline leaders, and customers, then shape a vision that stakeholders want to strive for.

---

2   Dr. Bob Rotella, *How Champions Think: In Sports and in Life* (New York: Simon & Schuster, 2016), 109.

The true power of any vision is the commitment, not compliance, of ground-level employees to understand it, believe in it, ideally be involved in making it happen. Frontline leader buy-in is essential for any vision to come to fruition. A common-sense way to earn that buy-in is through communication and involvement in the vision, goal, and strategy process.

If a clear vision is not alive and well on the frontline, the organization will stand little chance of ever achieving it. No matter what level of the organization you are at or what you are leading, having a vision is critical. Without a compelling vision, you will have to rely on people following you blindly. You may get compliance, but you will struggle to win people's commitment. They need to be in on it to want to enact it. Without their inclusion, their commitment is doubtful.

Frontline leaders and employees need to know what the future holds and what is possible for them within that vision. As a frontline leader you also need to appreciate how critical your role is in understanding, internalizing, and achieving the vision. Simply put, it needs to paint a compelling picture of the future and be meaningful for employees, no matter what their position or title.

Everything you strive for in the organization rolls up into this vision. It gives reason, purpose, and context for strategies, decisions, and innovation. Your own vision of what is possible should generally align with other leaders and the company as a whole. This requires sharing, listening, and understanding the vision that is in place and perhaps tailoring it to you. Ask yourself, "What is my role in fulfilling the organizational vision? How can I adjust my current practices to better serve this vision?"

Examples of organizational visions:

Disney:
to be one of the world's leading producers and providers of entertainment and information.[3]

---

3   Alex Williams, "Walt Disney's Mission Statement and Vision Statement (An Analysis)," Panmore Institute, last modified September 20, 2023, https://panmore. com/walt-disney-company-mission-statement-vision-statement-analysis.

Microsoft:
At Microsoft we are dedicated to advancing human and organizational achievement.[4]

Amazon:
"To be earth's most customer-centric company; to build a place where people can come to find and discover anything they might want to buy online."[5]

If you are a frontline leader, imagine how the above examples would influence decision-making, helping define the path that you and your team take. For example, if you are at Amazon and discover a customer being treated poorly, the coaching becomes pretty straightforward. The vision should be a guidepost for all leaders including frontline leaders. Where disagreement on a path exist, ask what is our vision and which path serves it better?

Study and understand your company's vision. It can steer you through much uncertainty, particularly if you are not being led in an ideal way yourself. Few can argue if your decisions and behaviours are aligned with your company vision.

If you are truly at odds with your organizational vision, you have options: 1) accept it and go through the motions through compliance, 2) lobby passionately to improve it, or 3) find an organization that fits you better.

I find it shocking when I ask clients, particularly those closest to the action, to describe the vision, goals, or even general direction of the organization. I often get a blank stare and/or a description barely resembling the official vision. It is clear to me that the vision printed all over the walls and media is really not influencing decisions and strategies and is merely ideological babble left over from the last executive retreat.

---

4   "Our Company," Microsoft, accessed May 17th, 2024, https://www.microsoft.com/en-us/about/company.

5   Daniel Pereira, "Mission and Vision Statement of Amazon," The Business Model Analyst, February 27th, 2023, https://businessmodelanalyst.com/amazon-mission-and-vision-statement.

In absence of a working vision, leaders must operate in a vacuum. If they are not clear about where they are going, this leads to firefighting, short-term thinking, and chaos. When time and resources are not applied consistently to building and embedding the vision and aligning activities with it, organizations and people fall short of their potential. Whereas some organizational visions can be vague, organizational goals are usually practical and tangible enough for every leader to embrace.

The issue with lack of vision or goals on the frontline is that it creates an environment that requires micromanagement. Some who are promoted into leadership positions have the mindset that "Workers don't really understand what we are trying to accomplish, where we are headed, so I really need to be involved in every decision." Ironically, frontline leaders detest micromanagement themselves. The way out is to be crystal clear on the big picture and vision. Even in organizations where this is fuzzy, leaders can and should be curious and press senior management for clarity of direction and then share that with their teams.

Vision clarity allows frontline leaders and their teams to creatively find ways to best achieve their goal. Absence of clarity creates uncertainty and a stressful guessing game. "How best can we reach our goals?" becomes the primary question to put before frontline teams. Ideas, ingenuity, creativity, and commitment tend to flourish when this approach is taken. This is true because leaders are challenging their teams to bring their top game as experienced professionals. Being included in solutions and coming up with the best ideas is inspiring and brings out the right kind of competitiveness in people. How many causes have you thrown your support behind where you did not feel some personal connection to the ultimate vision of where you are trying to go and what you are trying to solve? The workplace is no different. Employees need to understand what the goals and vision are, why they are important, and, in particular, why their role is so important.

Spending time and effort on this may seem unrelated to day-to-day success. True, in the short run. Organizations are often far too focused on the short run at the expense of the medium and long run. Wouldn't it be better to spend time on maximizing today's outcomes? Today's success is obviously important, but who is thinking about medium or long-term success? As a leader, that is part of your job. Below is an excellent framework to view various leadership responsibilities and behaviours.

Stephen Covey, author of *The 7 Habits of Highly Effective People*, frames the problem of reactivity versus proactivity.[6] Vision and goals are very much non-urgent but absolutely critical for business success. They are important, but not urgent. Frontline leaders who dedicate some of their time and energy to big important matters, like goals and vision, that are not a crisis are more likely to feel in more control and will be more likely to align with senior teams. Focusing some time and energy on the big picture, aligning with the organizational vision/goals, will likely require team members to handle more of urgent/Important activities. If you are stuck on a treadmill of urgency, crisis, and reactivity, you are certainly not alone but realize this approach has serious potential for stress, burnout, turned off teams, and increased need for micromanagement. There is a better, more balanced way to operate that will build better, more resilient, and high-performing teams.

Crisis mode dominates too many organizations and although they may be successful, they are successful in spite of this approach, not because of it. You may be saying, "But we are making X millions of dollars and the doors are still open, so what is the problem?" Well, perhaps the company is positioned well in a market that should allow X millions times three, or you may be successful now, but what happens when the market becomes more and more competitive?

A tip to taking a first step toward taming this hamster wheel of activity is to take a look at your calendar for next month. Make several one-hour-block appointments with yourself to spend time on what Stephen Covey termed quadrant two activities.[7] Preserve these appointment times and dedicate that time to non-urgent activities that are essential, things you need to be more proactive on. For instance, reviewing budget performance proactively before your boss does, walking the floor of your facility, building relationships in non-crisis mode, giving feedback (catching

---

6   Stephen Covey, *The 7 Habits of Highly Effective People* (New York: Simon & Schuster, 1989), 19.

7   Covey, *The 7 Habits of Highly Effective People*, 43.

people doing things right), employee 1:1 sessions before they are due or there is a crisis. By doing this, you will start to gain control of your time, your team, and your results. Preserve a little more the following month and so on to a point where you balance well between being a very proactive leader and also one that can navigate a crisis but with your team right beside you!

Spending time proactively discussing and sharing the organizational vision, adapting it for local circumstances, gives people a greater sense of purpose, and involving people in the discussion makes them part of the vision. This dedication of time and resources has a huge return, as it means winning people's commitment, which is always a good investment if you want to accomplish anything meaningful.

A famous NASA vision in the 1960s, put forth by US President John F. Kennedy, was "To send an American to the moon, and to return (the person) safely, by the close of the decade."[8]

It was not hard to get behind that compelling, time-sensitive vision and, by all accounts, it guided much of the decision-making and activity at NASA in the sixties. Many of the interviewees who helped frame this book cited clear vision, where are we headed and by when, as being a critical foundation for meaningful leadership.

An example of the power of this vision on people is when President Kennedy was touring a NASA facility and came across a person who clearly looked to be a janitor, and asked, " "What is your job here?" The man responded, "Mr. President, I am here to put a (person) on the moon!"[9]

A clear vision provides a guideline for stellar strategies, critical decisions, and creates a necessity for great behaviours. It makes work have purpose, connects people on a common path, and brings efficiency to an organization. A clear vision makes a frontline leader's job easier and

8   John F. Kennedy, September 12, 1962 Speech at Rice University, "We Choose to Go to the Moon," Wikipedia, Accessed May 19th, 2024, https://en.wikipedia.org/wiki/We_choose_to_go_to_the_Moon.

9   Kristen Michele Olson, "'I'm Helping to Put a Man on the Moon'; Communicating Higher Purpose in the Workplace," *Open Access Theses* (2018), 55, accessed May 19th, 2024, https://docs.lib.purdue.edu/open_access_theses/1432.

attaches a higher purpose to work at every level. Every decision can be filtered through the question, "Will this get us closer to our destination?" It is also critical for creating teamwork; if everybody on the team understands the vision, there is a much greater chance of people acting in unison. Importantly, a clear vision makes it easier to say no to many strategies and crazy ideas. In a world where many are overly busy, saying no is increasingly important both for organizational success and personal work-life balance.

People want to be part of something bigger than themselves and, particularly, bigger than their boss's next whim. By having a clear vision, and being transparent with it, leaders can create a shared and meaningful journey for their team. If anybody strays, including the leader, others can help them stay the course. In large organizations, a lot of time, attention, and resources are dedicated to developing a vision. It is then "rolled out." Whether or not enough of the right people were included in developing the vision, frontline leaders need to own it and interpret it in a concrete way for the benefit of their team and to achieve the right results.

It is not necessary or desirable for every leader in a large organization to develop a unique vision. A general vision is likely already in place. The key for frontline leaders and employees is to completely understand the vision, get aligned with it, ask questions, truly own it, and share their beliefs about the destination with their team. Communicate regularly and tie important decisions, results, and performance feedback to the vision.

Too many frontline supervisors and workers are unaware or disinterested in the vision and goals forming the direction of the company. In some cases, they don't know how critical their role is in supporting the greater cause. When this higher purpose is revealed, it is motivational for many, and results and commitment levels tend to improve.

Imagine your uber athletic friend invites you for a run. You just start running and talking and as you round a bend you both see a village on the horizon, about four kilometers away. Your friend suggests that you run to the village. No problem. You continue on your way. When you arrive, you round the traffic circle in the town square, then start on your way back. At that point, your friend sees a shiny statue high above the village that can be reached via a rugged trail, with a couple of rope sections to assist with the climb, and asks if you want to check it out. Reluctantly, you agree, even though your legs and lungs are already starting to scream, and you are terribly thirsty.

After another hour's slog up the hillside, you are taking in a beautiful view while slumped against the statue, hands on knees, panting and trying to catch your breath. Your friend then points out another village in the other direction and suggests you head there next. By this time, exhaustion, thirst, hunger, and anger set in. You push back. "Look, I had no idea we were covering the whole county today without water or food, and I am just not prepared for this. I'm going back to the village and catching a cab. You can do what you want!"

In this example you as the follower expect more transparency. You need to know the route, the vision, in order to be better prepared to survive and thrive on the trek. Everything from preparation, packing the right nutrition, and pacing would change depending upon the vision or destination. If it were a five-kilometre, flat route on easy trails, your preparation would be vastly different than if it were a twenty-five-kilometre slog through steep, technical, and challenging terrain. It is no different for your organization. The extent to which members/employees understand the vision of where you are going, why it is a worthwhile destination, and what their own critical contribution is, the more successful you will be in keeping people engaged on the journey.

Do you have a crystal-clear understanding of the vision and its rationale for your organization? That is step one for becoming a successful frontline leader. Don't worry if others around you or even your own supervisor are in the dark about the vision. Get curious about it, and enjoy the benefits.

CHAPTER 2
Follow Through

Promises are cheap. What people expect is colleagues, leaders in particular, to act on any promise given. As a leader, even casual promises are taken very seriously and many underestimate how much they will be both listened to and how firmly they will be held to account. Overpromising erodes trust and respect. As a frontline leader, you represent the organization and when people are promised action, they have high expectations.

I have heard frontline workers say, "My boss lies all the time." When I ask them to explain, they respond with something like: "Well, last month he promised he would look into getting us better gloves because our work area is hot (i.e., welding), but nothing has happened." Meanwhile, I know that particular supervisor has followed up with the safety department and been in touch with the procurement department to source better, more durable protective gloves. The problem is, that while action is being taken, it is not visible to the people the promise was made to. To many, that is the same as a lie.

In order to maintain integrity, a promise could include a check-in follow-up step. "I will investigate better gloves, keep you up to date with progress, and encourage any ideas from you in the meantime." This would be more of a concrete commitment than "I will take care of the glove situation." The transparent and successful approach to action should satisfy the worker, while the latter sets the supervisor up to disappoint. It is also a good practice to take note of every single promise you make and if you know you can't make it happen, do not promise that you will.

One of the greatest sources of missed follow-through is routine meetings. A typical company meeting will wrap up with responsibility assignments for creating action. Names, dates, and actions are logged, so all of these commitments become part of the official record. Too often there is a lack of follow-through on those formal, documented commitments. For example, Bob pledged to deliver engineering drawings at the next weekly meeting. When the time came, however, not only did he not provide communication about the drawings, he didn't even attend the meeting. Nothing in the way of follow-up or consequences happened to Bob, so you can imagine what that did for his credibility, his supervisor's credibility for lack of accountability, and for the level of team function.

Some supervisors will avoid the situation above by committing to the bulk of actions themselves, knowing full well that they cannot possibly do it all. Meanwhile many other competent people sit back amused and watch the supervisor become overwhelmed. Much of this self-inflicted pain stems from cultural norms that encourage a can-do attitude among leaders. It also has to do with discomfort and distrust in people and/or an inability to coach, delegate, or hold others accountable. Don't be that dumping ground for your team. It will crush you eventually and will do nothing to create fulfillment in meaningful work for your team members.

Often, frontline workers complain about being underchallenged and not reaching their potential, while their supervisor is overwhelmed. Overloading yourself as a leader erodes your credibility when you cannot live up to your promises. Good intentions to take care of things for your team will backfire when you become someone who cannot be relied upon. Your word will mean nothing. You will become untrustworthy. Thankfully, this is fixable if you are A) willing to trust others, B) don't mind sharing interesting and rewarding work, and C) are willing to put your ego aside and say, "I can't do all of these things, but collectively we can." The benefits you will see are numerous: reduced stress, reduced workload, growth for others, a more well-rounded team, and better results! This will not only balance your workload, but it will engage and inspire your team!

When you are next in a meeting and see an imbalance of responsibility being assigned, challenge it. For example, you could interject, "Mary has put her hand up for eight tasks and the rest of us have nothing? Who could best spearhead each of these items so that the plan is more balanced and does not all hinge on Mary, one of the busiest people on our team?" When this imbalance occurs, it is a sign of overreliance on position or expertise and an under reliance on team. While it may be true that Mary, holding everything else equal, would be the logical choice for the task, everything is not equal. Mary, as the supervisor, is overloaded and others may have idle capacity, including creative ideas. A better balance of duties and actions creates challenge, learning, and collaboration, all things typically lacking for many who are unfulfilled at work.

Everything in moderation, though. People have to fulfill their primary job responsibilities first. Discretionary time and interest can be used to help the team and the organization. In emotional intelligence language, this is called social responsibility in the workplace, that is, helping others outside of your formal responsibility area succeed. For some this is standard behaviour, and for others it needs to be encouraged.

An example of this is cleaning the sink after use on an aircraft. Airlines post a sign because social responsibility is not in muscle memory for many. Nobody wants to see a disgusting sink, but some fail to see their role in keeping that sink clean. Conversely, movie theatres have been training social irresponsibility by allowing us to throw our food and drink waste on the floor for workers to clean up later. While it is critical for leaders to follow through on promises and deliver on short-term commitments, it is also critical for leaders to protect against imbalance. Just say, "We are going to accomplish this as a team! What portion would you like to take on?"

I'm sure you have a friend who has good intentions but continuously falls short of their stated commitment. "Hey, I'll give you a call next week." Next week rolls around, and no such call occurs. What is going on is that people are excited to please others in the moment and will do anything to maximize that positive rapport. As far as overcommitting, that is tomorrow's problem. The issue with this as a frontline leader is that your credibility gets seriously eroded over time. Credibility is vital for success at work and in your personal life, and it can have dramatic consequences. People will just plain stop believing anything you say. The impact on career and social success can be profound. Keep. Your. Word. If you do, you will become that exceptional, rare Best Boss Ever to your team.

We are surrounded by tools and technology to address this problem. Rather than wasting memory on your multitude of promises, write them down immediately, put them in your calendar, a notebook, whatever. I see too many people in meetings promise the world without even bothering to jot it down. Writing it down can alleviate stress, as you spend zero energy worrying about forgetting it, and it also sends a signal to your colleagues or friends that you value and respect what they are saying and are serious about doing your part.

There are many benefits to being known as the one person who can be taken at their word. When you follow through and communicate how things are progressing as you go, you are essentially saying to the other person or group that they are important and your promise to them is your commitment.

There is nothing worse than someone listening, nodding yes, promising to follow up, and then failing to do so. You might as well just say, "What you said is not valued, and I am not going to waste my time on it." Great leaders exhibit that their word is more than just a suggestion; it is a contract. As Benjamin Franklin put it: "Promises may get thee friends, but non-performance will turn them into enemies."[10] It is far better to under promise and over deliver. It is a common leadership and human trait to want to please.

If you follow through on every single promise, you will inspire others to make their own commitments to help you and your team succeed. It is straightforward common sense but uncommon in execution, and it is a game changer with teams! I have seen groups either thrive or implode based on this one simple, controllable factor—FOLLOW THROUGH ON EVERY COMMITMENT.

---

10   AZ Quotes, accessed May 19, 2024, https://www.azquotes.com/quote/592160.

CHAPTER 3
Clear Communication

You have expectations of your team, and they have expectations of you. How clear are those expectations, and are you aligned? Never make assumptions about expectations. People see things from their own perspective. Express clearly what you need and expect from people, write it down and, importantly, make it a discussion. The more you link expectations to organizational needs instead of your own needs, the more success you will have. Seek their commitment, not merely their compliance.

I cringe when I hear supervisors say, "Do this task for *me*." It's not about you and that is not respectful communication! They are doing the task in service of the organization or goal, not their boss. They are not your slave. Something like: "I appreciate you taking on that aspect of the report; I would not be able to write it like you could!" will build a person up, while "I need you to do this for me" demeans them, with the subtext being, "I have power over you, so do this or else." It is not helpful to manage by threats and leaning heavily on position. This will lead to disenchantment, job coasting, and possibly turnover. You get the point. Everything you say is being put through a high-standard filter where people expect clear, respectful, inclusive communication, not a series of barked orders.

A bright, young supervisor asked me one day, "What do you think I need to do to climb the ladder in this company? I like my job, but one day I want my boss's job." I told her she was asking the wrong person, and I suggested she make an appointment to establish clarity with her boss and ask:

- What qualities in a frontline leader are most critical to you and to the organization?

- What skills and experience will be vital should I want to advance in a way similar to what you have done?

- What do you believe I should work on improving immediately?

- What medium or long-term things I should work on?

By asking these questions, the supervisor became crystal clear on what skills they needed to develop, what specific outcomes mattered the most to optimize role performance. After that, aligning herself and her team with the most logical priorities became easy. This process often works top down through formal performance review processes, but nothing should stop any employee from regularly getting clarity or verifying priorities and expectations from their supervisor. Taken a step further, reflect on all the tasks and expectations that you and others believe are associated with your position. Have your supervisor rank that list with you. Then if you get overwhelmed, you'll be clear on what is essential.

One barrier to this wise practice is people don't want to look weak or needy. If this helps, it actually makes the supervisor's job easier because they are likely unclear what each person's interpretation of key responsibilities and priorities are. Think about how clear you have been with your own team and with individuals about your expectations. If you are thinking this should be covered in an annual professional development plan, or in a formal job description you are right, it should. The problem is the formal annual review is frequently designed as a sales pitch for gaining a share of the salary increase/bonus pot. The roles and responsibility document is frequently a departure from current training, mentoring and practice.

Goal and priority clarity are often compromised when reward systems value innovation for the sake of innovation instead of delivering big on the base business. Ask for clarity. How important would you rate innovation and cool side projects versus attaining monthly objectives? Ensure your team know what you value and what is unimportant.

Having ongoing regular check-ins with individual team members, on a human level, regardless of mandated process, will ensure absolute clarity for all. There will be no surprises on the annual review. If you are thinking, *Wait a minute, I barely have time for annual performance reviews let alone more frequent check-ins,* think again. You are a leader. Your number one job is to support and develop your people. They cannot excel, in most cases, without your attention, guidance, clarity, and support. Whatever you think may be more important, it isn't more important than your people. The other reason to act now on clarity is that behaviour change in the right direction leads to better results today rather than waiting for next quarter or next year.

Bob just got hired as the manager of the quality department in his mid-sized manufacturing firm. He has thirteen individual contributors reporting directly to him. Bob has a clear idea in his mind about what a good employee will do and won't do. As Bob is new to the organization, he alone knows his personal values/standards. This is a major and typical gap. Another issue is that Bob does not have a clue about how these thirteen people expect a manager to behave in order for them to maximize their success as part of the team. It is a two-way street, where neither Bob nor his team members hold all the cards.

Through a series of one-on-one and group discussions, Bob and his team arrive at standards for each to uphold. In order to work through and arrive at an optimal operating culture, it is important that Bob and his team understand what they need in order to maximize the working relationship. One example they agreed upon is that process innovations are valued highly and minor mistakes in the learning process will not be judged too harshly; they will be viewed as learning opportunities. Everyone, including Bob, knows their role in creating a high-functioning team.

Too often mixed messages, like "innovate" and "don't you dare make mistakes," create a conservative environment, where people steer clear of the pain of a mistake by hanging on tightly to the status quo, avoiding creativity/innovation, and even holding back on brilliant ideas and extra effort. All bad things!

In most organizations, formal job descriptions exist. Although these documents typically contain huge lists of task responsibilities, they often are short on specific leadership values that clarify what your role as a leader truly is. They are also frequently outdated. It is always a good practice when onboarding to have several discussions about the contents of the job description versus the actual expectations for stellar performance. Even if this step happens long after you start your role, getting alignment on your job or role description is worth the effort for the sake of productivity, ease of decision-making, and confidence in your path. As a frontline leader, understanding fully the formal obligations of your team members that may reside in collective agreements and/or roles and responsibility documents is paramount. Great leaders will understand and leverage these sources to fuel employee growth, development, and team success.

Communicating well during team meetings is a major point of stress for many supervisors, new and old. Team meetings are a huge opportunity for alignment, engagement, and motivation. Facilitating team meetings comes easy to some leaders but if you are not one of them, here are some points to consider:

- Get them involved and talking

- Do more asking and less talking

- Prepare by having an agenda

- Post the agenda ahead of time when possible

- Have handy any policy related to the topic of the day

- Ask open ended questions such as "How can we best incorporate this plan into our business?" Get them thinking and solving!

- Share results, good or bad but especially good

- Acknowledge others

- Own what you deliver (that means understand the intention and rationale behind whatever you are asked to deliver to your team- don't complain about it) *Complaining down,* aligning your work team against management or outside parties on policies or decisions, simply demonstrates to your team that:

- the company is aligned against us
- upper management are incompetent
- you, our leader, are completely powerless in this organization

- Always ask for suggestions, concerns, feedback with open questions like "What impact do you see this change making in our daily routine?"

- Meetings should create action and the responsibilities should be spread throughout your group. Note the action, who is responsible, and when it will be reported back (i.e., next meeting, March 6)

It is not your job to stand in front of your team and speak at them for a half an hour. It is your job to lead (facilitate) a discussion to make progress on the topics covered in the meeting. Also a good idea to nominate a scribe and share the notes and follow up as needed to check for change, support implementation, resolve any concerns.

CHAPTER 4
Persistence

Every business has setbacks, barriers, failures, and down periods. Strong frontline leaders see beyond those difficult times and are an inspiration to others. It's not about which particular setback occurred but rather how you react that really matters. It is easy to behave well, be kind, generous, and upbeat when things are going well. Leadership is better judged when things are going sideways in a chaotic environment. Maybe there is dysfunction between shifts, undo pressure to perform from above, or poor cooperation and buy-in from below. Difficult events can either paralyze or mobilize people. It is both a choice and a challenge to be a steady, guiding hand navigating and inspiring the team through adverse conditions. While going through adverse conditions, great leaders find the time to acknowledge progress, however small. This is motivational.

Persistence stems from confidence and belief in the overall purpose of your organization or department. It requires a great deal of patience. Persistence is made easier if you are committed to a clear organizational goal or vision. We are achievement-oriented creatures, so when we sign up to support a goal or to lead and initiative at the annual retreat, it becomes personal. As we nod our heads in support of the plan/goal, we are committing to it.

For example, a frontline sales manager for a raw food ingredient supplier gave her word that she and her team would secure a leading share in the sports soft drink sales segment by the fourth quarter. That particular market experienced an unforeseen downturn in demand. Navigating quickly to seize the opportunity, the manager got board approval to reduce pricing for a four-month period in order to help prospects trim costs by switching ingredient providers, providing they signed on for two years. Client issues became supplier issues to help solve the problem, and the marketing director secured an all-time record market share relative to established suppliers, albeit at reduced margins. As markets recovered, the customers stayed and the persistent sales team far exceeded budgets in a tough market year.

In the example above, the persistent frontline leader became very curious about specific issues and creative about solutions. She was the optimistic voice in the room to rally her team rather than sitting on her heels and waiting for the market to turn around. Prospect/client contact and support during the difficult times would be remembered when selecting suppliers for future contracts.

Persistent leaders find a way to support and develop their team members. They view setbacks and mistakes as a routine part of the learning process. Trust cannot be blind, so persistent leaders will have a firm grasp on what competency gaps exist and provide the right support for successful skill building to reach the goal.

Persistence is about casting excuses aside, navigating around obstacles, and creating teamwork to rise to the challenge. This can be mistaken for bullheadedness. The difference, though, is that persistence is targeted at achieving a goal and being open-minded about how best to reach it.

> "Nothing in this world can take the place of persistence. Talent will not; nothing is more common than unsuccessful (people) with talent. Genius will not; unrewarded genius is almost a proverb. Education will not; the world is full of educated derelicts. Persistence and determination alone are omnipotent."
>
> —Calvin Coolidge, thirtieth president of the United States

Persistence is an essential quality for any leader. It means the difference between shining or crumbling when unforeseen circumstances arise. Persistent leaders are thinking of the long-run consequences of their decisions, not just about immediate concerns or rewards. I have heard too many frontline leaders say, "We have a unionized workforce and can't really do much when they do not measure up." Persistent and successful leaders that have also established excellent rapport, have developed mutual respect, somehow seem to be able to address performance issues regardless of collective bargaining arrangement. Further to that, great union leaders dig in their heels and coach individuals when performance issues threaten their livelihood.

A discussion about persistence would not be complete without mention of Colonel Sanders (Kentucky Fried Chicken). After retiring, penniless, at age sixty-five, the Colonel hit the road selling his "finger-licking good" chicken recipe to restaurants for a small residual of the sales. His first sale happened on the 1009th sales call. The obstacle of "no" was not a deterrent to his goal. He knew he had a great idea, and it was a matter of finding a like-minded restauranteur to take a chance on him.

This example can easily translate into your own workplace when upset conditions inevitably occur. It is your decision to either use the upset condition as an excuse to abandon your goal, or you can ask yourself, "What is the best result or way through given this setback?" Great leaders will calmly involve their team in answering that question. Great leaders know the team will succeed. They don't just sit back and wait and see.

For example, a facility has a production line with planned production of ten thousand units per day. During the second hour of production an unexpected jam-up occurs at one of the workstations, causing thirty minutes of downtime for the entire line. Since it is a ten-hour shift, the team is now five hundred units behind. As the leader, you can either throw your hands up and say, "Don't worry about today's goal; it's out the window." Or you could rally the team by saying something like: "Well, we were slightly ahead of the daily-run rate when the downtime occurred, so it is not as bad as it looks. What are some ways we could make up the unit shortfall and still achieve our ten thousand–unit goal over the remainder of the shift?"

It may seem obvious to take this logical approach, but it is all too common to see the goals abandoned at the first hint of adversity. In fact, in poor performing teams, the leader may not even share the ten thousand goal with the workforce, which is a whole other problem. The leader's persistence is critical but unless the persistence is also embedded in team members, sub-optimal performance will be assured.

Great leaders understand the power of their team to creatively navigate and make the most of whatever obstacles arise. Involving frontline workers in such creativity and involving them in the goals also improves engagement and a sense of accomplishment on the job.

Persistence is critical component of grit. Grit, a combination of persistence, belief, and ambition, according to Angela Duckworth, author of *The Power of Passion and Perseverance,* can be summed up like this: "I won't just have a job; I'll have a calling. I'll challenge myself every day. When I get knocked down, I'll get back up. I may not be the smartest person in the room, but I'll strive to be the grittiest."[11]

The ability to keep slogging when there is little sign of hope can be difficult, but it is also inspirational. Grit is the salesperson who truly believes that their product can solve real problems for buyers and is willing to take a hundred "no thank you" responses before finding the one enlightened person who sees the value. In any leadership role, grit is vital. There will be obstacles, barriers, push back, and setbacks with any goal, plan, or vision. Some of your mentors/co-leaders may try to dampen your optimism and you will be wise to let the pessimism roll off of you without overtly challenging them. Show them, don't tell them. Your ability to function, remain calm, and persist when someone or something is standing in the path of your goal is vital.

For example, we were doing a standard organizational culture assessment, and our first job was interviewing each department manager and a significant portion of the plant employees in order to gain insights into the culture and leadership impact. We divided the interviews randomly among our three coaches. One of the key personnel on my colleague's list was scheduled to be away on vacation. This colleague is a person with tremendous grit. She realized that it would be impossible to interview the leader onsite, as the person was leaving for vacation the next morning.

---

11 Angela Ducksworth, Grit: The Power of Passion and Perserverance, accessed May 19, 2024, https://www.goodreads.com/quotes/7742181-i-won-t-just-have-a-job-i-ll-have-a-calling.

Acting quickly, my colleague asked if she could pick their brain for a few minutes prior to their flight, stating that the assessment would not be the same without their valuable input. Feeling rather special, the leader agreed, and the critical interview was completed.

This was extraordinary within our team and for our client. It was established right away that our team would do whatever was necessary to deliver the best results for our client. The grit demonstrated to get around the obstacle helped establish early credibility with the hard-working people at the organization.

Making mistakes is a natural part of any learning process, but too many leaders shy away from innovating or trying anything different for fear of failure and being judged. You need to understand that errors happen during development, including leadership development. Michael Jordan once said, "I've missed more than 9,000 shots in my career. I've lost almost 300 games. Twenty-six times I've been trusted to take the game winning shot and missed. I've failed over and over and over again in my life. And that is why I succeed."

Michael Jordan demonstrated persistence and grit. I had the good fortune to witness this superstar's persistence in person. After struggling in the first three-quarters of the game, and an untimely post-basket taunt by the opposition guard, Jordan and his Chicago Bulls found a new gear and dominated the fourth quarter, coming away with a commanding victory.

Grit is an attractive quality possessed by people who don't mind working and, at times, grinding it out to achieve results. I want people with grit on my team and in my life. I know, if I drop the ball, they will be there fighting to get it back. You have likely known people that are just doers. They don't make excuses, they simply get on with things, doing the most they can with the resources they have. These people are essential to any great team, and the leader needs a certain amount of grit in order to win the confidence and respect of their team.

A cautionary note on grit. There is a fine line between being gritty and being overly involved. It is far better for leaders to inspire their team to be gritty by modelling those behaviours as a leader than for the leader to be the only one with grit and take over team members responsibilities. In the latter circumstance, the leader might horde all the interesting, challenging work, micro-manage, or be a lone wolf. None of these qualities help build a great team.

A gritty leader is one who will find a way to make the team win, in spite of obstacles. One prerequisite to grit is being absolutely convinced that the vision, goal, or plan is a worthwhile one. If you are only mildly keen on the goal, the first small obstacle may be a welcome excuse for not accomplishing what you started off to do.

For example, if the company goal is to improve productivity by 10 percent, a production issue, that seems out of your control as a frontline leader, may cause you to abandon the need for efficiency. Here's how. Production shut down for one hour because of a mechanical failure during the shift. Instead of trying to gain back as much productivity as possible in the last portion of the shift, you just abandon productivity for that day. You really believe the status quo productivity is fine and corporate leaders are just greedy. You are not in alignment with the goal.

On the other hand, if it were explained that 10 percent productivity improvement would allow the doors to remain open for the foreseeable future and anything less would mean closure, you would have a different view on one hour of lost productivity. You would likely move mountains to rally the team to higher performance, find out how to prevent maintenance glitches going forward, and find a way to hit the 10 percent improvement in spite of the downtime.

The point is, fully utilize your grit and your team's grit, become curious about the vision, goals, and plan. Ask why the goal is important for you and your team. Share that information with your colleagues. Be part of the solution, and make it happen. Own the goals and your team will also own the goals. You will be more successful, as will your team. You will build a reputation as a leader who gets things done and needs to know more than "just do it" for a reason to put in extra effort, and you and your team will be held in high esteem within the organization, and with outside stakeholders.

CHAPTER 5
Confidence

Leaders who have great confidence in the organizational direction and of people to get the job done stand a much greater chance of inspiring others. Believe in the possible. Once you believe in what you are leading, others will stop asking "why" and start asking "how." Ideally, they will be suggesting "how best" once doubt about the path is set aside.

Confidence comes from a belief in your ability to succeed based on experience. I am a mountain biker. From time to time on a trail, we encounter "skinnies," narrow wooden structures elevated off the ground that we ride down when the regular trails are too mundane. Skinnies can be daunting for even experienced riders. There are established fundamentals for riding on them, such as always keeping your eyes well out in front so that you can visualize the best track down the middle of the wood and with that focus prevent going off the edge.

But where does the confidence come from? Positive related experience is a great starting point. Mountain bike coaches will train you on a no consequence, ground level plank, then slowly graduate you to narrow, sketchy, elevated skinnies. Along the way, your positive experiences cement the idea that you have got this, and your assurance grows. The coach also has confidence in you because they have the experience of seeing many others struggle and succeed at the same task. The key on the skinny is your absolute confidence that you will triumph.

If you were to look off to the side, that is likely where you would end up, all cut and bruised. By focusing your mind on the goal of getting to the end of the skinny, you can relax. This positive self-talk is part of confidence building in both sport and life.

As a leader, coaching others, it is critical that A) you believe they can accomplish what you are asking, B) you give them whatever support/ training/coaching they need to succeed with confidence, C) you do this at the right pace, and D) you ensure you do whatever to instill a belief in the person being coached that they can do it. Be patient and keep in mind, as Oscar Wilde said, "Experience is the name we give our mistakes."[12] Confidence in your plan and your people allow you to overcome obstacles on your journey. Building confidence in others through constructive feedback will, over time, build the unstoppable productive team you want.

Of course, in order to have confidence in others, you have to trust and believe in them. Great leaders I have worked with tend to have a high regard for those they lead. In fact, many say that their leader has more belief in their abilities and potential than they do themselves. This typically inspires people to try their hardest to live up to the image created by their leader, producing higher levels of achievement and commitment than would otherwise occur.

Have you ever wondered how an individual or team performance can rise to the occasion as pressure of competition or a deadline mount? In 1984, I rode the ski chairlift with recent US Olympic champion Bill Johnson. We were both going to the top of Whistler to take our turn on the downhill course; I was forerunning it (up and coming racer/victims sent down the track in advance of the competitors to ensure it is safe). Bill and I had known each other for a few years, attending many of the same races, so I felt comfortable asking how he was feeling about that day's race. His response is still etched in my brain. He said, "I am going to win," and a big smile came across his face. Yes, it sounded very arrogant, but Bill did win that day. He did not always win, but he always believed he could win. I have always wondered what proportion of his victory is owed to his remarkable belief in himself.

---

12 AZ Quotes, accessed May 19, 2024, https://www.azquotes.com/author/15644-Oscar_Wilde/tag/experience.

What Bill Johnson had was undying confidence in his ability to deliver the goods under pressure, which he did over the course of a couple of years. When he won, it was clear that his confidence was a major factor in his success.

Does confidence have the same impact in business? If you, as a front-line leader, can convince yourself that your team will succeed and they become convinced as well, minor obstacles will not easily delay you or them for long. There will be no stopping you and your team! Once you are able to accumulate a few wins, the confidence with grow. Conversely, defeatist thinking will also have an equally big but negative impact on your results as a team. Everything you do and say, positive or negative, has a magnified impact as it spreads through team members. Expect to succeed, plan to succeed, navigate obstacles together, and you will stand the greatest chance of success, no matter the endeavour.

Remember, "Whether you think you can or think you can't, you are right."[13] (Henry Ford) This belief in the possible is essential if you lead anything. Even as those around you are giving up, try to see the best possible outcome and inspire others to get there!

---

13   Quotespedia, accessed May19th, 2024, https://www.quotespedia.org/authors/h/henry-ford/whether-you-think-you-can-or-think-you-cant-youre-right-henry-ford/.

Inspiration

CHAPTER 6
Listening

We were born with two ears and one mouth. Being a great frontline leader has more to do with truly hearing others and meeting their needs related to performance than imparting wisdom. It is about helping others reach solutions, not determining them yourself. Good listening sends a strong signal that the other person is valued and respected and it prevents them from coasting.

In a traditional command and control leadership approach, the worker would be the one listening, not the supervisor. The supervisor would be dispensing orders and instructions; no listening required. Under that approach, little is expected of the worker in terms of creativity, ideas, input, or commitment. Command and control will usually produce uninventive, apathetic followers. While some can become very content and deliver good work, few will ever thrive and reach their full potential.

Leaders who ask more and tell less will harness not only better solutions and ideas, they will generate more effort, commitment, and results from team members and they will also learn a lot more. If you have been taught to dispense instructions, making this important shift will take some effort. Initially, even great open-ended questions (that is, "How do you see improving our reliability on this product run?") may elicit a response of silence. It may be very uncomfortable until the person realizes they are expected to think.

Someone who has become accustomed to being spoon-fed instructions/solutions will be challenged initially. This is a worthwhile change and can be a relief for both the leader and the worker. The leader will find relief in this approach because once they go down this path, they will realize, not everything is on their shoulders. They are surrounded by talented, smart, experienced, and capable people. The worker will be relieved because they will be a critical source for good ideas, and they will feel appreciated and needed. This positive mindset has a beneficial effect on engagement, effort, creativity, company culture, productivity, and retention.

Good listening requires that you are calm. Before sitting down with a direct report, it is helpful to clear your mind and put other distractions, such as your phone, to the side. That alone will tell the person that you value them. Whatever topic you are hoping to cover, realize that the biggest opportunity is getting the person's opinion, ideas, and commitment. Ask, ask, ask, and truly listen to their viewpoint. Once they deliver an answer, it is often useful to ask them to go deeper.

For example, if I wanted a solution for an upcoming critical order, I might ask, "What are some ways that we can ensure we deliver this on time, most efficiently?" The initial response may be, "Well, I think we should pre-stage it now for departure next Thursday." Rather than telling them that this is a good idea, you may say, "Tell me more, particularly how and where you would pre-stage, given our space limitations and this week's orders to consider?" By doing this, you are helping people not only see the big picture but influence it. This typically makes them feel smart and valued. When you make people feel valued, you will unlock their commitment.

There is a lot written about the value in using open questions. Open questions get people thinking and involved, as in the shipment example above. This is often lacking with leaders who are hanging on to a top-down leadership style they were mentored to use. Somehow they have come to believe that their role is exclusively telling others what to do and, worse, how to do it. It is entirely possible that you may have been mentored by such an individual yourself. Be very careful adopting that style. If you as a leader stick to the path of telling others what to do, there will be no shortage of situations that will require your attention. Everybody will be awaiting your instructions instead of getting on with the job. One underrecognized side effect of the telling approach is that you will encourage coasting. Why should people contribute their best if their leader is involved in all important decisions?

Imagine if every worker only did what they were asked instead of using their experience and common sense to do the right thing at the right time. Not good. This behaviour is what you are asking for if you choose the micromanagement, top down, telling approach. Free yourself by adopting ASK more, TELL less.

When people feel valued, they tend to strive harder, help others, and be net contributors. If you want highly productive team members, listen to what they have to say.

Good listening requires laser focus on the other person. Nod occasionally in agreement. Gain clarification without interrogating the person. Look at them. Be interested. Body language counts as well. Be relaxed yet attentive. Make sure the space is neutral. Sit on the same side of the table. Get out from behind your big fancy desk, if you have one. Be as disarming as possible. Take notes, unless you have a perfect memory! It also sends a signal that you are listening and find what they have to say important enough to capture.

If you want to build a stellar team, consider these words by Karl A. Menninger: "Listening is a magnetic and strange thing, a creative force. [Those] who listen to us are the ones we move toward. When we are listened to, it creates us, makes us unfold and expand."[14]

What is it that makes listening especially difficult in the workplace, in spite of all of the benefits explained above? Some obvious barriers are set goals, mandates, rules, policies, procedures, and an overall rigidity of organizations. Why bother asking for opinions if we already know what will be done? This is a bad excuse for lack of listening. In fact, given the abundance of structure, restrictions, and complexity in organizations, it is even more important to listen carefully for more thoughts and ideas about how best to incorporate restrictive rules and policies and still succeed. It may be more about *how* things are done than *what* things are done. No

---

14   Palena R. Neale, "Deeply Generous Listening Takes Practice," Psychology Today, April 13, 2022, https://www.psychologytoday.com/ca/blog/leading-success/202204/deeply-generous-listening-takes-practice.

matter what barriers, restrictions, or limits are in place, creating dialogue that is aimed at navigating the best outcome is always better than dictating behaviour. This starts with listening well. If listening is important to you, you will find a way. In noisy, industrial settings, finding a quiet spot for a quick discussion will send a message that you care about what others have to say. This goes a long way with people. They will engage with and move towards pleasing leaders who make them and their opinions a priority.

CHAPTER 7
Curiosity

One quality of great frontline leaders is curiosity. Being interested in other people's viewpoints signals humility, respect, and makes them want to help in the cause. It also tends to make them feel valued which in turn raises their effort and their output. Some of the smartest, most successful people I have met are very curious. They are lifelong learners and just want to know things. As a result, these leaders gather a lot more ideas and solutions and learn more about their team. A learner's mindset is refreshing in a leader, especially in an experienced leader.

Yet, I have met a lot of leaders who do not exhibit much curiosity at all. They rely more on assumptions and past experience, guided by their own gut and expertise. That can come across as lazy and arrogant to those being led. I have come to understand that lack of curiosity can stem from a dated belief that asking questions is a sign of weakness or lack of confidence. In a sense, their ego stands in the way of learning and building a highly engaged, more successful team.

But what if the whole reason I got promoted to this supervisory role is that I do know all the answers? Stop right there. You may know all the answers according to you, but others may have different perspectives that may lead to even better outcomes. If you keep open to that possibility, you will not only find superior solutions, but you will also build more committed, satisfied employees. The worst thing you can do is compete with your direct reports on subject matter. Let them have their say and if they are wrong, ask open-ended questions to help bring them around versus directly challenging their position. For example, "Can you explain how you see the product withstanding that increased temperature?" versus "Our product will never stand up under those temperatures."

The first thing in being curious is to focus on them, their experience, goals, and ambitions. Take a genuine interest in the person. Instead of illustrating every scenario through your personal experiences, pay attention to theirs. Be curious about their perspective and their related experiences. It is so tempting when a person relates their experiences to jump in and match or outmatch their story with your own. What you are essentially doing is competing with them, showing them who's boss and looking down on them. You are basically saying, "Well, that's nothing, let me tell you about when I was in your job."

How inspiring is that? It is harder but better to ask a follow-up question, such as: "What was that like?" or "How did they react?" and continue to listen. One of the best questions/statements I have heard and used extensively is "Tell me more." That really gets a person to open up and shows that you care about what they have to say.

How curious are you with team members? Think about times when you felt listened to and someone was very curious about you. What did it do to your attitude, mood, and behaviour? How will you remind yourself to be more curious? Some methods I have seen work before a meeting are to plan a few questions ahead of time (that is, What can I learn about this person?), draw two ears and one small mouth on a whiteboard across from where you are sitting, or have a colleague monitor and then give feedback on your level of curiosity.

When curiosity crosses into the personal realm, human connection tends to be enhanced. Here we are talking with people about things they truly enjoy, like hobbies and families. Showing interest in these areas is typically appreciated, providing it is done with tact, is seen as authentic, and no personal boundaries are breached. Many of us were taught to draw a very firm line between personal and business. In other words, colleagues are not friends and vice versa. The problem with being detached, cold, uninterested, and completely business-focused is this approach only appeals to the analytic/logical side of people. That is a fine approach but as Dale Carnegie put it:

"When dealing with people, let us remember we are not dealing with creatures of logic. We are dealing with creatures of emotion."[15]

Curiosity will help you understand the whole person, including their interests and any prejudices, which will build a trust that will likely help in the course of normal business and when any challenges arise in the workplace.

In order to start down the path of being more curious, asking appropriate, open questions and truly listening to the responses will be key. After a conversation with someone, ask yourself what percentage of the talking you did. If the number is high, think again about how you can balance it out going forward.

If done well, curiosity on work matters will send a signal that you are interested in others' perspectives/solutions, and you expect creativity and results, not just adherence. This will take time until people realize that you are not going to do all the problem solving, and you will be relying on them as professionals to find the best path. Some will be stunned by your about-face, but they will be honoured to be asked.

Even if you think you know the clear answer to a problem, how many assumptions are you making? Getting curious will allow you to test your theories and even if others confirm your viewpoint, they will be grateful for being asked.

Like any leadership trait, curiosity can be overplayed. We have all been in that uncomfortable conversation with somebody who is overly curious, and it can feel a bit like an interrogation. Ideally, you can simply learn a bit more about colleagues gradually over time rather than flooding them with questions in one sitting. There is no hurry. You will likely be working with them for a long time.

What is surprising is that you can work with people for many years and yet know very little about them. It enriches the work relationship and connection enormously when you know some of what's happening in their life, their hobbies, interests, family, and so on. As a leader it can also

---

15   Brainy Quotes, accessed March 20, 2024, https://www.brainyquote.com/quotes/dale_carnegie_130727.

help when considering how best to recognize a person. For example, a family pass to a museum may not be an appropriate reward to give a single person or vice versa, offering a single pass to someone with a family.

Curiosity brings understanding; it requires setting aside assumptions and facing people and situations with an open mind. It may be that you were put in charge because you know a lot about the subject matter in your organization and are in a good position to impart wisdom and dispense orders. There are two problems with that approach. The first is that it turns people off. Who wants a know-it-all for a boss? It makes people coast and give up. Secondly, you don't learn anything and, yes, there may be even better ideas and approaches than you know.

Without a certain amount of curiosity and innovation, the organization will stagnate. Life as a leader is more interesting when you are learning. You also increase the buy-in and effort of everyone on the team, improve productivity, and maximize results through this approach.

CHAPTER 8
Empathy

Empathy is about appreciating the other person's perspective, situation, challenges, and experiences they bring to the team. It is different than sympathy, and it is not a weakness! One learned friend suggested I change the word "empathy" in this book because it is soft and getting old-school leaders to embrace it will be difficult. I have faith in the abilities of leaders (even antiquated ones) to adopt new language for understanding others when it helps their team.

I have witnessed first-hand over my entire career, old-school leaders adapting and changing for the better. In fact, many suspected "tough" leaders are actually pretty caring individuals who have been misguided on how to succeed as a leader.

Many leaders have been fed the notion that they need to be strong, intimidating, decisive, and demanding of other's respect. Think about the best leader you have ever had. By best, I mean the one that made you want to try harder, learn more, and be a better colleague. Were they more empathetic or more intimidating?

It is important to note that empathy is not an excuse for lowering expectations; it is understanding the unique challenges and obstacles that will need to be considered for a given person to achieve the goals set out. If you still aren't convinced that caring and empathy are essential leadership qualities, remember these are two things absent in both psychopaths and narcissists. A few psychopathic and narcissistic individuals fool their way to the top, but that does not make it a worthwhile approach.

Building an amazing team requires taking others' perspectives and challenges into account. Similar to curiosity discussed in the previous chapter, you must suspend judgement and your own agenda while exploring what is happening for the other person. That is easy to say and hard to do. One key is asking open questions/statements such as: "Tell me more about that," "What do you find the most daunting about this?" or "What impact will this new policy have on you and your team, and how do you feel about that?" If my boss cared to ask these types of questions, I guarantee you I would walk over hot coals to help them and the organization win.

A lot has been written about gender differences in regard to empathy. You guessed it, men typically have less. The stereotype of the caring, supportive, empathetic woman and heartless ego-centric man has truth, but counter examples can be found for both. For leaders this should only be viewed as a starting point, and it is where you end up that really counts. In North American culture, men are starting at a deficit, so they are wise to advance their level of empathy if they want to have success with people. I have also seen women, who have advanced in male-dominated workplaces, display as little empathy as their male counterparts.

Things are changing as workplaces demand more emotional intelligence (which empathy is a large part of). This change is painfully slow, if you consider that *Emotional Intelligence: Why It Can Matter More than IQ* by Daniel Goleman was published in 1995. The common sense, insightful findings of Goleman's work would suggest vast improvements toward more emotionally intelligent leadership approaches. In practice, these more humane and inspiring leadership approaches are far from common. Change has been painfully slow as leaders hang on to old leadership approaches geared toward the 1950s mindset. I have seen over and over the damage caused by leaders who act in a way that can only be described as emotionally daft. Behaviours such as jumping to conclusions, assuming the worst in people, and excluding key knowledgeable people in decisions and opportunities are alive and well in the modern workplace.

Emotional intelligence is the next evolution in leadership and follows the Theory X (authoritative) versus Theory Y (participative) work initiated sixty years ago.[16]

Some signs that a leader lacks empathy and/or faith in their direct reports include:

- Publicly humiliating employees

- Taking credit for others' ideas

- Using "I" instead of "we" when highlighting successes

- Asking employees to do work for "me" instead of for the organizational goals or the team

- Solving problems themselves versus harnessing the talents of their team

- Being overly busy and stressed, while their direct reports are under little stress or challenge

- High department turnover or discontented employees

- Demotivated employees

- Infighting among team members

- Poor department performance

Contemplating this list should spark interest for leaders to consider the impact of their current leadership approach, including emotional intelligence abilities. Fortunately, emotional intelligence can be measured. Unlike IQ, which is rather static, emotional intelligence skills are more modifiable. Leaders can learn more effective interpersonal approaches and how to manage emotions that influence decision-making and stressful situations.

This is one area where lifelong learning is essential. Whether you are at the start of your career or nearing the end, continuously improving your

---

16   "McGregor's Theory X & Theory Y: Definition and Manager Types," Study.com, accessed May 19, 2024, https://study.com/learn/lesson/theory-x-theory-y-management-types-examples.html.

level of empathy for others will pay dividends. Specifically, people will want to be around you, will more readily commit to whatever goals you have, and you will be seen as a team player. Further incentive to hone empathy and other emotional intelligence skills is it will enhance family, friends, and broader social relationships.

Our workplaces have valued technical and subject matter expertise and credentials over one's ability to work with others, build a team, and lead a winning culture. Knowing technical things and being able to operate well as an individual contributor better than others has been the exclusive key to securing leadership positions. Ironically, some of the very best individual contributors have a very narrow and technical expertise that has little to do with their ability to get along with others, let alone inspire them or build a team. They are good with solutions, technology, and equipment but often at the expense of excluding others' talents and contributions. This leads to a very top-heavy team where the boss knows it all and everybody plods unquestioning along behind.

Organizations have valued lone-wolf hero-type employees and promoted them into positions of leadership and greater influence. It is not surprising, though, that these leaders lean heavily on their own skills, knowledge, and ego, and they often fail to win the respect and commitment of their team. They struggle more than most with humility, a key ingredient for great leadership on the frontline. It is not a truly viable option for any leader to be a lone wolf, no matter how much experience and knowledge they have. If you are one such leader promoted for subject matter expertise and great solo contributions, a fundamental shift must occur from a focus on yourself to a focus on others if you want success.

Some organizations are considering emotional intelligence (EQ) abilities when hiring and promoting, but it is certainly not yet a norm, in spite of the fact that leader EQ is strongly associated with unlocking maximum commitment and effort! Simon Sinek in *Leaders Eat Last*[17] describes how US Marines, without being ordered to do so, line up at the mess hall in reverse order, putting the most junior members first and senior leaders

---

17   "Leaders Eat Last: Why Some Teams Pull Together and Others Don't," Inkwell, accessed May 19, 2024, https://inkwellmanagement.com/books/leaders-eat-last.

last. The idea is that if you value people by putting their needs above your own, they will give it their all!

Many organizations cling to the notion that exerting authority over people to keep them in line is the way to achieve results. It does not matter if the leader has an engineering degree from the most prestigious school and understands the workflow better than anybody else. If they can't show empathy, include and respect others, and show humility, they can never inspire others and consequently nor can they maximize an organization's potential.

Application:

Alissa has brief, informal individual weekly meetings with her team of seven process engineers, which is a mix of new and experienced members. Alissa asks each person for an update on their work, gets a report, then gives non-judgemental feedback. She also casually asks about life in general to understand the person outside of work. Conversely, people on her team ask about Alissa's outside interests and passions. These meetings flow back and forth, with Alissa aiming for a conversation that leaves each person feeling valued, trusted, and counted upon.

Indeed, people feel an essential part of this great team. In team meetings, Alissa is interested in and expects opinions from everybody. By simply guiding individual conversations in an inquisitive but non-intrusive way, Alissa has received the best 360 reviews in the company and furthermore, the engineering department has improved productivity and quality dramatically since she took over.

Interestingly, Alissa takes on less actual detailed work than her predecessor, a detail-oriented, stressed-out lone wolf, who would typically handle all the complex challenges. Alissa puts the difficult matters before her team to solve and is not only outperforming her predecessor, but she is building a resilient productive department and influencing future leaders for long-term sustainability. Knowing her team members well has allowed Alissa to leverage strengths within the team, challenge people, and overachieve on department goals.

I have seen examples such as this play out countless times when leaders decide to shift away from autocratic styles toward greater empathy and other Emotionally Intelligent approaches. Soft skills get hard results! Skills, education, street smarts, and know how are all important for frontline leaders, but they are not sufficient. People skill sets incorporating Emotional Intelligence enhance a leaders influence because people will want to work hard for leaders with these priorities. These skills are all learnable and will provide endless challenge and reward for frontline leaders who want to truly maximize their potential as well as their team's.

CHAPTER 9
Belief in Others

As a frontline leader, your belief in others is one of the best tools in your toolbox. I learned this lesson as a budding ski racer. I was a very passionate skier from the age of three, but, in my mind, I was not yet very competent at the age of twelve. I just felt lucky and excited to be part of the ski team with like-minded kids.

There weren't many of us on our small-town team, but we had a very inspiring coach who had just moved to the area. Some of the first races that season were not highly successful, with many of us placing near or at the back of the regional pack. It was discouraging, but our coach did not waver in his belief in our ability to succeed.

He was excellent at giving feedback without demoralizing me. In fact, he assured me that with some work, I had the potential to win these very races. I was not really thinking like a winner after coming nearly dead last, so it was exactly the advice I needed to stick with practice and continue racing. He also said it would take hard work, dedication, and openness to his coaching to make this a reality. I was inspired to try my hardest because of his belief in me. I'm sure I was not alone in receiving his confidence, but it didn't matter to me. I was going to improve and succeed. I had nothing to lose, so I bought in.

His belief in me made me train harder, be open to feedback, and filled me with more confidence heading into subsequent competitions. I spent all the time I could training, both on the snow and off. I even joined a weightlifting club at about age fourteen to accelerate my overall strength for the ski-racing season. We lifted weights from five a.m. until the start of school at eight-thirty, five days a week. I was driven by a higher purpose.

I really had no idea about my potential, and it took him pointing it out to make me think it possible to excel. Thanks to his encouragement, I did exceed my own expectations as a ski racer. His belief in my capability had a lasting impact, not only on my athletic pursuits but also academic, business, and life in general. I have had many coaches in my life and truly believe the most important thing they can do for a person is to help their team members believe in a brilliant future and help them define a clear path for it.

Belief in others is paramount in the workplace. As a leader, you are surrounded by skilled, talented people, who are full of potential. Many of these people may not see clearly what they are capable of. One of the most important roles of any leader is helping people grow and develop. Fundamental to this growth is a belief that a person can break through to a new level, improve, and thrive beyond where they have settled. Obviously, there are limits to a person's capabilities, so being realistic and helping them take just the next step is prudent. Once the person has some success, their own self-belief will start to kick in and help them on their path to their full potential.

There are simple ways to signal belief in others in the workplace, and it can be very powerful for both the person and the results. For example, take two managers, Jill and Andrew. Jill is willing to have her team members try and fail, and she trusts their judgement to know their limits and when to ask for help. Jill has no problem delegating interesting and challenging problems to her team and then having them work it out for themselves. Whether things go perfectly or not, Jill supports her team members and stands behind them. She is curious and sincerely seeks others' opinions on real problems facing her or the business. This is a signal that she values and respects people. She also says things like "I am not worried about you creating some great solutions given what I have seen so far."

Andrew, on the other hand, has a dim view of the competence of his team members. Anything complicated stays on his desk, and he is not tolerant of errors, even if they are minor. Andrew's delegation involves distributing run-of-the-mill work and demanding compliance to his way of doing it.

From the above, Jill's direct reports are growing more, are involved in interesting work, are challenging themselves, and giving more of their discretionary effort. They are more fulfilled at work, more productive, healthier, and happier. Who wouldn't want to have Jill for a manager or for a direct report? Trusting and believing in people pays huge dividends. The obvious baseline requirement for this impact is that people are provided adequate training and mentoring to be competent. In my view, lack of competence in people is rarely as much of an issue than lack of confidence in people.

Leaders often underestimate the knowledge, skill, and potential of their direct reports, which is a waste of human potential and a drag on workplace performance. Believe in people and help them reach for the stars. It is good for everybody, and the results will pay dividends for all.

The other implication of not trusting or believing in others is that less-trusting managers are overly busy taking care of matters that really should be handled by their team members. This has dire consequences, including delayed decisions, lack of attention to their own role, lack of focus on higher-level priorities, and a demoralized, less committed, less productive workforce. It can also take a personal toll including stress, burnout, and even clinical depression. I encounter overstressed, overworked leaders at all levels in my everyday work. A common thread among those burned-out leaders is that they see themselves as essential in every situation. They are supreme micromanagers that have a lower regard for their direct reports and tend to be overly focused on immediate results versus long-term results.

Instead of believing in and supporting their team, some leaders chose to be the hero to the point of taking credit for their employees' work. It is unfathomable how they see stealing thunder from their people as a prudent strategy for building a strong team.

An important perspective for successful frontline leadership is to see yourself as support for a brilliant team. Your job is not to outsmart them, outshine them, or put your stamp on everything. Your job is to believe in them, help them grow, recognize their strengths, and accept that they will falter as they grow. Setbacks are a reality as growth and learning occur, so being tolerant is important. You will build a highly competent, motivated team and when the results are clear, be sure to credit team members, not yourself. You will not need to spend time trying to make yourself look good or stand out. Your team will own the results and anybody worth pleasing will see your impact. Your humility, combined with stellar results, will build a sustainable powerhouse of a team.

If you are wondering what is in it for the team members who will be challenged to do more, consider the following: often, workers are under stressed and are not stretching themselves intellectually because the frontline leader is doing all the decision-making and all the interesting, challenging work. Many workers have said that they are bored, under challenged, and at times feel they were hired from the neck down. Just do the job and leave the thinking up to the boss. This robs the workforce of fulfilling, meaningful work.

The good news is that this is reversable when frontline leaders commit to staying in their own space and trusting and even demanding that the workforce to utilize their skills and talents to the fullest. In other words, spread the workload. It sends a great message that people are trusted and respected as professionals. Individual fulfillment in doing meaning-ful work, higher engagement, improved team performance, and a less stressed-out supervisor are all the benefits when this path is chosen.

CHAPTER 10
Coaching

Coaching is pretty easy to do and very difficult to do well. It is a fundamental role and responsibility of any leader yet many leaders underutilize this important tool. This is particularly true of leaders new to leadership or even new to their role. Why not? Part of the answer is that there exists a widespread assumption that to effectively coach, one needs to have subject matter mastery. From that standpoint, the coach simply finds faults and tells people what to do.

This "tell" form of coaching is appropriate in select circumstances such as a when a brand-new worker takes instruction from a highly experienced manager with deep technical knowledge in the business. This is what many people think coaching means. This top-down style would promote wiser, more experienced leaders telling less experienced workers what to do and how to do it. If this gap in experience is present, there is a brief period of bliss where both the coachee and the coach are fulfilled under this "tell" approach. It quickly loses the desired impact as soon as the person being coached starts gaining competence and confidence. From that point onward, a more effective way to lead is through "asking" great questions and engaging those being coached in a conversation to identify and close gaps.

In addition to getting the coachee involved and creating their own plans to improve, great coaching involves giving feedback effectively. Athletic coaches have long understood this. Video review sessions clarify the exact level of performance against known standards. Athletes can see exactly how their efforts were effective or not. There is no arguing with the facts on a video. Referees also use video to support of refute facts surrounding their critical calls. In this sense feedback is really just fact. Great coaches can deliver factual feedback in a way that is compelling and even motivational for their coachees.

Imagine a manufacturing line product change over. There are long lists tasks with a particular sequence in order to have a smooth product changeover to the next product. In good manufacturing facilities these changeover sequences are just part of standard operating procedures that are both embedded in the habits and posted for all to see. Let's say for example a team, with pretty experienced workers had a turnover that was double the expected time and data revealed that steps 1 and 2 were mistakenly reversed. In this simple example, the leader of the team could A) simply tell the team members to do their job better and do it correctly going forward. This approach is efficient but one must question how much commitment it builds. In this situation, the coach does all the talking while the team members remain silent, idle, and subservient. Another approach is B) give factual feedback about the situation and invite the team member(s) into the conversation and allow them to provide the solution or commitment. Approach B requires more trust but has a much higher probability of true buy-in. Approach B could look like this:

> Coach/Leader, after a pleasant greeting: "I noticed on today's changeover report the target time was doubled and there was mention that steps 1 and 2 were reversed for some reason." It is important after delivering these basic facts that the coach stops talking and pauses.

> Team member: "Actually, I was at the doctor's during that time but Marcia informed me what happened. When Les correctly paused the line in advance of the changeover, the computer automatically sequenced 2 before 1 for some reason. Les has IT coming in later this afternoon to ensure we are operating to standard and that our 4:30 changeover goes to plan."

Note that approach B does not make any assumptions about why results were a certain way, just that they were. In keeping with just the facts, tone of voice and body language are best kept neutral as well. Imagine the carnage approach A would have on the relationship between the coach and the coachee in the changeover example. The worker being coached was not even at site and it was a computer issue not a behaviour or commitment issue. Approach B is impactful and engaging and if there is a behavioural issue it puts the coachee in the driver's seat for closing the gap. The goal is to get their commitment through a respectful conversation, not make a commitment for them. Pausing to let them commit is key. This takes a tremendous amount of patience but once you get it, it is highly effective.

Pinpoint coaching[18] is a simple, effective model used by thousands of leaders to improve the effectiveness of giving feedback and create productive coaching relationships.

---

18   Westwind Leadership Inc., trademark, 2024.

Although the model is simple, it is challenging for many leaders (coaches) to exercise enough patience to PAUSE to allow their coachee to step into the conversation. Pinpoint coaching flips the responsibility for action from the coach to the coachee. Think about who needs to be responsible and accountable for the results or behaviour change. It is the employee being coached. Pinpoint coaching is aimed at gaining their commitment to improve. The employee's own commitment represents their word, their personal contract and it is a lot more powerful than their boss's wish or dream.

> Boss: "The machine quality score was 69 percent this morning Bob." PAUSE
>
> Bob: "Let me see the details of the report. I like to achieve 95 percent as a minimum."
>
> Boss: "Sure, as you can see the current customer order run requires minimum thickness of 2 mm on every sheet. The results show that nearly half of the sheets at this machine were scanned as under-sized."
>
> Bob: "Whoa! I know the problem. I was under the impression we were still running for XYZ, which was 1.5 mm. My apologies. I must have missed that detail in the start-up meeting and I will correct it immediately. Can we use the off spec for another order or should I scrap it?"
>
> Boss: "Thanks, Bob. Glad we discussed this early in the day and we can likely use it for an upcoming XYZ order next week. Have a great shift."

In this illustration of pinpoint coaching, when Bob said "I will correct it immediately," it was really a personal contract. This is way more powerful that his boss telling him to get it done or to improve his performance! It is the difference between commitment and compliance. If you have a choice, commitment is always more effective and sustainable than compliance.

How well did the boss do at just sticking to the indisputable fact(s) "quality was 69 percent"? Who made the commitment, Bob or the boss? What do you think the chances are of a successful remainder to the shift? Notice that the problem got addressed without the Boss telling Bob, the professional, what to do. The Boss simply made an observation, then shut up and allowed Bob to step in and get to the bottom of things and commit to the change. This is also a lower stress, productive, inspiring way to lead because Bob will feel respected while being challenged to improve.

If Bob decided to put up a fuss, in the example above, the boss could simply reinforce the known standard as a starting point to gauge Bob's commitment. If that failed to generate a commitment, the boss could use her positional power and simply tell Bob what to do. This latter option is suboptimal and should be reserved for when there is unreasonable pushback.

A very important point about feedback is that great leaders devote the energy to catching people doing things right. In the example above, Bob was caught out in a poor performance situation. Importantly, the boss should follow up and catch a couple of great quality reports and give Bob feedback. This step of catching people doing things right is often skipped because it is a bit more uncomfortable and/or the supervisor is too busy responding to other negative events where feedback is mandatory.

When giving positive feedback, the PAUSE can add value as well. The PAUSE just lets the person into the conversation and that can be helpful even when the results are positive. For example, "I see the quality is hovering around 100 percent this week!" PAUSE. "Yes, I was embarrassed about last week and have been really focused on that run information in each morning meeting." In this case, it helps the person to commit further simply by expressing why they have improved.

Managing up with tactful and factual feedback is less risky than trying to tell your boss what to do. If your own boss does not exude all of the great leadership qualities outlined in this book, it is likely stressing you and others out and causing distraction, productivity and possibly commitment issues. Many people suffer through bad bosses, complain about it to everyone else but nobody has the courage to address the issues head on. Unfortunately, everyone loses and the boss can never grow. The concept of *direct deal*, where you deal with the person directly first before ever discussing your concerns with others, is important to consider. For example, if your boss, unknowingly, displays double standards, this will have serious implications for their credibility and their influence. Imagine that he is routinely late for your weekly supervisor's meeting and at one of those same meetings he has on the agenda worker tardiness! It would be easy to chuckle to yourself and make fun of him after the meeting room with your peers. How much would that help improve his behaviour?

The direct deal approach, incorporating feedback as outlined under pinpoint coaching, would be straightforward, providing you have a solid relationship with your boss. "John, during the meeting you emphasized the importance of time integrity among our workforce. I could not agree more and will do my part. But you arrived ten minutes late for our own meeting!" PAUSE.

John: "Oh my goodness. That must have looked silly. Thank you so much for letting me know. I am so sorry and if you will excuse me, I have an apology, not an excuse, to make to the others." Whether or not John loved the feedback, what do you think the likelihood of him waltzing into the next supervisory meeting late will be? The alternative, talking to others about it, changes nothing and is just office gossip. Note, John thanked his direct report and viewed the feedback as a gift. Just because someone is higher up the ladder does not mean they don't deserve the gift of feedback. We are all constantly improving or should be.

Lead by Example

CHAPTER 11
Fairness

Have you ever experienced favouritism? Whether you are the favoured or the jilted, it is not a good feeling. People who are favoured may feel guilty, while those who are treated unfairly may feel disheartened and give up. Favoured people tend to coast and not put in much effort. Afterall, they just need to show up. Those not favoured are typically unmotivated, as working hard is not recognized in comparison to their level of contribution compared to favoured colleagues. Why would you bother doing anything exceptional if you are not appreciated? In both cases, suboptimal performance will occur. Favouritism does not work for anyone in the long run.

I started my career thinking/hoping that workplaces were merit-based, but too often I have seen that is not the case. For success in the workplace, it clearly matters who you know, who you are related to, and who you emulate as to how successful you can be. This is so wrong, and organizations that operate with this as a cultural foundation typically underachieve. Leaders at all levels are in the best position to challenge this damaging norm. It takes courage where favouritism is deeply rooted, but it will feel right and also pay big dividends.

Assertiveness plays into the favouritism equation as well. Attention and favour are given to those with the loudest voice. It simplifies the choice for promotion or feedback or reward. "I noticed Mary doing all these good things but never heard from Richard all year. I think Mary is more deserving than Richard." Meanwhile, Richard may have contributed higher quality and valuable work but did not advertise his deeds.

Austria is dominant in the ski racing world. They have turned out champion after champion since the inception of international ski competition. They have not exhibited a lot of favouritism. Your past is your past, and you will be judged based on current performance.

You may recognize the name Franz Klammer. He was the most dominant downhill racer of his time, winning a majority of the mid-nineteen seventies events he entered. Heading into the 1980 Lake Placid Olympics, he was the reigning Olympic champion (Innsbruck, 1976). In order to defend his title against the world, he had to face his own Austrian powerhouse first.

During qualifying, Franz Klammer lost out to four faster Austrians, including upstart Leonard Stock. Klammer was out, Stock was in. Stock was crowned Olympic champion in Lake Placid because the Austrians refused to allow favouritism, even for the most decorated athlete the sport had ever seen. Let the clock decide! The Austrians believed in fairness so much they were willing to bench Franz Klammer, Olympic and World champion and legend, in pursuit of their best shot at Olympic gold; it worked!

Favouritism is widespread in work cultures today. Just ask any employee. They will tell you of certain people who are on a fast track in their organization and are judged differently and sometimes given a pass on sub-par performance or behaviour. Excuses are made for faults and accountability is less for the favoured few. Why does this happen, how does it serve the organization and what does it do to the fabric of the culture?

Favouritism can happen for a variety of reasons. In some situations, the leader is supervising their friends or relatives. Some supervisors will do anything to preserve friendships or maintain rapport with relatives. In addition, some employees will take advantage of their relationship with a friend or relative supervisor to improve the relative ease of their work life. This can manifest, for example, when a supervisor routinely gives easier or more interesting tasks to the favoured and leaves the mundane and difficult or even dangerous tasks or responsibilities to others.

This habit of favouritism does not even pay off in the short run. It takes zero time for the rest of the team and organization to see through this approach, and the result is reduced productivity.

The impact of favouritism is large. By favouring the few, you are alienating the many. This has an impact on the level of discretionary effort and overall level of commitment. It is a two-way street; if you care about me by treating me decently, I'll care about you. If not, I will either leave, or I will quit but stay and be a drag on your success.

Many organizations take pride in promoting from within. That has many benefits. Reducing favouritism is not one of them. The risk of creating favouritism is increased for any promotion from within, especially when a work peer is promoted within the same department. The person being promoted may have well-established alliances and grudges with their former peers. It will be extra challenging not to let those relationships adversely impact the level of fairness in the workplace. For example, unpleasant work assignments could go to foes, while interesting, fun ones could go to allies. Everybody will see through this favouritism and consider it a leadership flaw. Sometimes even those being favoured see this as a bad way to lead.

Favouritism can also be revealed in the way poor performance or mistakes are handled. The favoured have few consequences, and the foes face the full extent of accountability. This is also viewed as weak leadership, and favouritism in handling poor performance is one of the most common and damaging flaws a leader can have. Virtually every time I encounter a disengaged workforce, leaders are practicing some form of favouritism and poor performance is being handled inconsistently. It is obvious to everybody, except sometimes the leader, and it causes many to lose respect for their superior and workplace.

If you have an underperformer on your team, everybody knows it and expects you as the frontline supervisor to deal with it. Any failure to deal with underperformance is seen as abdication of your responsibility. People will lose respect for you and the organization when you let underperformance continue. Turning a blind eye will just give you a black eye. Dig in your heels and address whatever gap you see with feedback and coaching as highlighted in chapter 10 on coaching. Your success depends on this. Handle this and you will win respect and commitment of the rest of your team. In addition, you will set standards that will be appreciated by all of the hard-working members of your team.

CHAPTER 12
Honesty

It is sad to have to include honesty in a leadership book, but after asking thousands of employees over the past couple of decades to name key qualities they admire in a leader, honesty is always near the top of the list. When inquiring what is behind this, employees relay stories about how they have personally been lied to or misled by their leaders. There is a gradient from bald-faced lies to failure to fulfill a promise to taking personal credit for work that their own team members accomplished.

It seems so obvious that being honest is a baseline requirement for any leader. If dishonesty exists, it is sometimes hard to filter out without doing some digging. You can't very well ask leadership position candidates whether they are a liar and expect a truthful answer. Liars will give the same answer as honest candidates. Nor will references or colleagues likely call out their friends when they know a career hangs in the balance.

Unfortunately, I see gaps in what is said and what is done every week. Leaders routinely say one thing and do another. For example, "I will share the strategic plan with you right after our meeting next week." Then they don't share it. "I will call you early next week." No call is made. Make it easy on yourself and maintain credibility by under promising and over-delivering. It sounds so obvious. The old proverb "the road to ruin is paved with good intentions" applies. A great way to turn your team off is to overpromise.

I have often wondered why on earth a person would set themselves up for failure like this. My gut explanation is that it has to do with a need to please people in the short term. Tell them what they want to hear. The immediate sensation is good, but once the promise is delivered it is soon replaced by guilt and disappointment. Eventually this leads to an erosion of credibility and trust in the leader.

The problem with this short-term bias is that your reputation and credibility are all about long-term consistency.

There are a couple of simple practices that can help with building trust, respect, and coming across as honest. One very simple one mentioned in chapter 2 is to always jot it down and better still is to enter the task into your calendar as a planned action. Another important aspect is to communicate back to the individual(s) that were promised the follow-up. This alone will build enormous trust. Tackling every single request or question yourself is a common trap for frontline leaders. When more limited commitments are fulfilled and followed-up combined with delegation, and just saying no in some cases, your perceived honesty and integrity will rise.

Trust is critical to any high-functioning team and honesty provides the foundation. That sometimes means leaders being humble, owning mistakes, and being transparent about concerns. These are all strengths, not weaknesses. Being a little vulnerable with your team will make you more human. Nobody expects their boss to be perfect but they do expect a boss they can trust. Many great leaders admit faults to their advantage. I believe people admire the willingness to own up to imperfection.

There is nothing worse than a leader that puts on a façade of perfection, never admits to errors, knowledge gaps or lapses in judgement, and tries to cover up all their faults. This comes across as arrogant and as dishonest, to the extent that employees know the underlying truth.

Leaders that clearly have faults yet fail to own them are highly likely to be considered dishonest. It is also true that people who are considered dishonest will fail at securing a commitment from their team.

Rapport, humility, and common ground are an antidote for suspicions of dishonesty but actual honesty is required to build trust. Taking an interest and understanding your direct reports and allowing them to get to know you is critical for building high trust relationships.

Spending unstructured time proactively with people on your team can accelerate rapport and trust and inoculate yourself against suspicions of dishonesty.

It sounds, simple: be honest, build rapport and gain trust. So why doesn't every frontline leader embrace this approach? One reason is personal image. Who wants their reputation marked with negative things like weaknesses, mistakes, failures and personal shortcomings? Only those who feel very secure in their role and/or a belief in the benefits of honesty and integrity will be secure enough to choose the high road. A lot of bad behaviour, including dishonesty, is routed in insecurity. Performance management systems may even punish leaders for acknowledging their sub-par decisions versus praising them for learning. My advice is rise above that insecurity and develop a moral code beyond those around you. As hard as it is to believe, honesty can be your differentiator in the workplace and your team will flourish for it.

CHAPTER 13
Reserve Judgement

Wait a minute! I thought the reason I got promoted was because of my good judgement! True, good judgement is essential. What I am talking about here is being too quick to judge people and their behaviours. The people you are leading are likely overly judgemental of their own behaviours without their boss wading in. So how can you effectively coach them to perform better? The quick answer is to help them reflect on their behaviour (good or bad) but give them the opportunity to plan and execute the path forward. You get them to commit to the right behaviour going forward versus you choosing the path for them.

Have you ever spoken with someone who is a great listener? It is an uplifting feeling and makes people want to unload all their best ideas and issues. Great listeners bring out truth and reality which allows people to move forward unencumbered. One of the essential qualities of a great listener is that they are curious and want to learn about you and your experience/story. They are not as interested in evaluating you as they are in valuing you and your story.

In reality, we are always judging others, and they are judging us. We do, however, have control over how and if we express those judgements. It takes self-control to not overreact to others by expressing all of our judgements and assumptions about their behaviour upfront. True listening is a state where we attempt to temporarily suspend judgement and let the speaker know it is safe to speak their mind.

Becoming less judgemental requires real effort for a lot of us. Our society has conditioned us to evaluate situations and people. We put people in categories, such as "us" or "them," based on observations and assumptions. This is convenient but can be damaging to relationships when overused. Recognizing the particular damage being judgemental has on relationships is the first step to reducing the amount of judgement you place on others.

Leaders who are overly judgemental tend to be feared rather than admired. Imagine if your boss said, "That Jim is always trying to impress everybody with all his new-fangled ideas for efficiencies, like I hadn't thought of them before!" How would that strike you? Many would see the boss as very judgemental, somewhat jealous, and someone who would freely talk about others behind their back. Would you wonder, *Am I being discussed like this when I am not here?* The net effect of being judgemental is that it repels people. How much truth would actually be revealed should such a leader try to get to the bottom of an issue?

Even if Jim was the only one in the room, it would still be counter-productive to judge and shut down the idea. For example, "We tried that already last year Jim and almost lost a key piece of equipment." Jim would understandably feel bad and be reluctant to step forward in the future. A better leader might say something like, "Tell me more, Jim. How do you envision this efficiency improvement making things better, not worse? What have others said about this?" This would allow a more respectful and complete consideration of the ideas and may reveal that Jim has considered upsides and downsides fully.

If you choose the path of judging everybody, you will paint yourself into a corner. Judgemental people will never be given the benefit of the doubt. Others will be looking for any minor fault, and they will be logging it. The old adage "people who live in glass houses shouldn't throw stones" applies.

The job of a leader is to help, develop, encourage, and support people, not simply judge and correct them. Now, this is not to say that feedback, development, and accountability aren't key. They are. It is all in how and when things are communicated, though. A key element of great leadership is to coach others to such a point that they are owning the goals and they are self-critical about any shortfalls. A simple reflection about factual results is often sufficient for feedback.

For example, as the key frontline supervisor of a clothing manufacturer you witness the weekly operations meeting. Afterward, you speak with Mary, the operations VP. "Mary, you declared in January that by second quarter you wanted all supervisors to report from the new template at the weekly meetings. I noticed today that we all used the template but Marcus did not." (Fact.) PAUSE. This simple factual feedback allows Mary to decide a course of action, hold Marcus accountable, without being told what to do. This approach is non-judgemental and will allow Mary to pursue *her* goal with support from her direct reports.

A slight difference in delivery would transform the conversation into a judgement-laden, stressful event. "Mary, I thought all supervisors were supposed to use the template? Why is this not happening, and what is with that Marcus character?" Which approach would motivate you more? Which scenario would make you work harder?

The importance of the example above is the locus of responsibility. As long as the responsibility sits with Mary to accomplish her goals, there is no need for being overly judgemental. Judgement is not helpful because Mary is already moving the team toward that goal. If, on the other hand, Mary is not really committed and just riding along following orders from her own boss, more judgement and harder accountability will likely be required to inch her and the team along.

In case you are thinking this is a soft approach to leading, think again. The aim of leadership is to inspire people to achieve goals. Being non-judgemental helps build stronger connections between leaders and those they lead. This connection increases the likelihood of alignment on goals and, more importantly, the chance of those being led sharing the ownership of the goals. For leaders, this should be good news. It's easier to be non-judgemental. There is less stress, less guilt, and better achievement. There really is not a downside. Some may worry, if I don't judge and micromanage, people won't do the required work. If this fits your mindset, it will require a shift.

More trust, less judgement will create conditions for others to commit and come on board. If you want to create this work environment, some questions to ask yourself are:

- Do I trust others or try to control them?

- Do I ask questions or simply give instructions?

- Am I curious, or do I tend to know all the answers?

- Do I consider what is important to others and make efforts to understand their perspective?

- Do I talk about others behind their back in a judgemental way?

- Do I believe I need others intellect, experience, and efforts to achieve our goals, or do I just need them to do what they are told?

- Do I listen to learn or listen to reply?

- Do people approach me for support or advice, or do they go to anyone but me?

The side benefit of being less judgemental is that there is reduced effort for the leader. Your input and involvement in every little matter will become less necessary as people take more responsibility for their own work, which will make your life easier. Don't worry if others will do everything exactly as you would, provided they achieve goals in a responsible and ethical manner.

Application:

Ask the person you are coaching or leading to give themselves feedback before you step in and do so. People are their own worst critic and are often hyper aware of any gaps in their own performance. Your job as a supervisor is not simply to critique them, it is to help them improve.

For example, one of your team members, Jessie, was asked to train the rest of your team on the new software that they were piloting over the course of two half-hour information sessions. During the first training session, you noticed that Jessie seemed very defensive about some of the potential navigation challenges identified with the software. This intensity disrupted the learning and was disappointing for all. After the session you ask Jessie to come to your office.

"Thanks so much for volunteering to pilot the software, Jessie. How did session #1 go from your standpoint?"

Jessie: "Well actually, I got really defensive over some of the questions people were throwing at me and I think that was counterproductive. What did you think?"

"Thank you. I agree with your assessment. I am happy you had the courage to step up and take on the project when it would have been easier to coast. You took amazing ownership over the software program and were defending it's every feature. Together let's review the purpose of the software and the purpose of the sessions."

Jessie: "It really is simply to speed up our shift end reporting and the purpose of the sessions is not to convince everybody it is great but rather ensure they know how to use the software. The decision to go in this direction was made. We are just trying to do a smooth implementation now."

"How do you think session two can get us further down that path?"

Jessie: "I think the best way will be to pick a volunteer and I will coach them through a shift end report from start to finish as a demonstration. We can handle any questions together as we step through the process."

Notice by the supervisor reserving judgement, Jessie was able to give herself feedback and also committed to her own solution. You as the supervisor just provided a few prompts. If you chose to reserve judgement, that does not mean that people will not be held accountable. You still have a responsibility to ensure that goals are achieved, teamwork is optimized, and workplace culture is improved. That requires addressing issues, but if you want that to be more impactful, you must involve those being coached in both their own feedback and ensure it is their commitment they are aspiring to.

CHAPTER 14
Integrity

Like honesty, it seems so basic to act with integrity. The difference between honesty and integrity is that integrity is a higher standard. Integrity requires high morals in addition to always telling the truth. For instance, you are a manager in a large company. You witness one of your colleagues taking credit for one of their direct report's brilliant ideas. If you are simply honest, you don't need to reveal the facts unless asked. If you have integrity, you will feel obliged to bring the truth to the surface, in spite of how much conflict it may create and how uncomfortable you may feel.

> "If you have integrity, nothing else matters. If you don't have integrity, nothing else matters."
>
> —Harvey Mackay[19]

Much of what you are able to accomplish as a frontline leader is based on the mutual respect and trust you establish with your team members. If you always act with integrity, you will earn the trust and respect of your team. You will also be modelling behaviour you want to see in others. This will have a cascade effect and make it a workplace that attracts like-minded people with integrity. This positive work climate will help you and your team accomplish great things. Whatever goal or challenge is

---

19   Brainy Quote, accessed March 20, 2024, https://www.brainyquote.com/quotes/ harvey_mackay_528768.

thrown in front of you, you will be more likely to succeed when you have a team of people that have each other's back and trust one another. People want to try their best for colleagues and bosses they like and respect. In order to create this climate, you as the leader must act with integrity.

Sometimes leaders breach integrity in favour of short-term personal gains. This never works out in the long run. Long-term success depends on sustained performance, which requires leaders to make decisions that place long-term team success above short-term results and self-interest. For instance, in a shift-work organization a supervisor can make themself and their team seem more productive by neglecting cleaning and maintenance activities in favour of a bit more production. Cross shift workers and supervisors will likely catch on to this short-term, selfish behaviour. Unfortunately, this occurs to this day. Leaders would be wise to avoid being sucked into the short-term mindset of urgency that dominate so many workplaces. Making the right, fair decisions is far more important than making fast decisions in favour of immediate results. Many leaders struggle with this as they try to measure up to established organization norms.

You will stand out if you have integrity. As Mark Twain said, "Always do right. This will gratify some people and astonish the rest."[20] It's a sad commentary on the average workplace that by simply having integrity you will stand out.

Colleagues and I have interviewed thousands of leaders and workers and from what they have shared that simply being honest and having integrity is a huge advantage. It requires putting what is right above what is right for you. Integrity includes admitting when you make a mistake, having humility, and acknowledging success in others no matter where or who produces it. Starting with integrity in mind will never serve you wrong and will establish a great work culture. It also may require unwinding some entrenched current practices.

As a leader, you are asking your team members to trust you to lead them in a direction that will make their work lives better. In chapter 1, the

---

20   Brainy Quote, accessed May 19th, 2024, https://www.brainyquote.com/quotes/mark_twain_122044.

importance of having a vision was explored. That vision is more of a delusion unless you are viewed as a credible leader on that journey. Integrity is at the heart of your credibility. Why would people believe in the big vision, goals, priorities if you continually disappoint on the small things? They won't. This is why being true to your word, not over-promising, showing up on time, and following up as promised are all so important.

When you are seen as a high integrity leader, you will earn the respect from up, down and across the organization. This has big implications for you and your team. It may mean greater opportunities, resources, and responsibility because who would not want to put their money and hope behind a team that delivers as promised with a leader that can be absolutely relied upon. When you lead such a team, it becomes a magnet for like-minded talent as well. When your team members, as part of this winning work team, are describing their work experience to outsiders they will be beaming.

Operating with integrity will make you stand out among your peers and will make them want to try harder and be better leaders as well. This will bode well for teamwork and organizational success. In this way, simply acting with integrity is like catalyst in raising the bar for everyone to achieve to new, unprecedented levels.

CHAPTER 15
Self-Awareness
(with a little help from others)

None of us fully appreciates the impact we have on others. This is particularly true of leader-worker relationships. If you are a leader, assume every action, every word, every joke, your tone, and your body language all collectively build your image, good or bad. Expectations are heightened when you are the titled leader. You have formal authority and you represent the organization so you are automatically held to a higher standard. This comes with both privileges, such as the power to make decisions, and responsibilities, such as making the right decisions and considering the impact on others when you do so.

On the downside, the sensitivity to leaders' behaviours can mean casual comments or laughing at the wrong joke are often seen as faults. When you are given the opportunity to lead, be aware that others are following your lead and are judging your every action with high expectations. That behaviour and influence should be positive, fair-minded, and full of integrity.

In many of the 360 reviews conducted over the years, I have been surprised by how unaware leaders are of how exactly they are perceived by their peers and direct reports. In spite of knowing and working with others for years, many leaders rate the impact of their own behaviours and contributions in stark contrast to what others think and feel. Typically, their self-image is more favourable than what others say and their self-awareness of reality is low. The people impacted by their behaviours often fail to give open feedback to the leader in question, partly because of conflict avoidance and partly because they fear repercussions, especially if they directly report to the leader.

Occasionally, I come across leaders with high self-awareness of where they stand with others in their view of themselves. What's interesting about that is having knowledge of weaknesses is often not correlated directly to efforts towards closing gaps on those weaknesses. "I know I am not a very good listener …" "What steps are you taking to improve your listening abilities?" "Nothing, it's just the way it is …." Really?!

Leader self-awareness, often the result of feedback or self-reflection, is only a starting point. This awareness, if acted upon, is instrumental in building a stronger team. Your ability to adapt based on awareness of opportunities will be an inspiration to others. The alternative, being inflexible and stuck in your ways, will be frustrating for others, and you will repel them.

You may have your team comply with your instructions, but you will be doing it solely with your positional power, which typically fails to secure their true commitment. If you believe your self-awareness is on the lower end of the scale, for example, you don't have a clue how much you impact others or how you are perceived, that is fixable. Once you believe it is important to be aware of your impact, improving the situation is straightforward.

You can simply ask others for feedback on specific instances, like: "In the update meeting this morning, tell me about how my overview was received by you and if you know, others. Was the rationale clear for our new direction? What questions do you have?" In other words, don't leave it to chance and assumptions. You may get interesting and helpful responses that will help strengthen your future ability to communicate effectively with the team.

An example of feedback that you might never receive unless you ask as above is: "Sarah, you used the words 'I' and 'me' too often throughout the update meeting. 'I want you to do this for me (because I am in charge)' instead of 'We are going in this direction because it will improve the likelihood of us hitting our annual plan and we all committed to that plan. We are a team here!"

If you are not aware of the subtle differences in those two statements and the big impact difference for the team, you may, despite good intentions, be undermining the potential for a stellar team. Some solicited, sincere, and proactive feedback from those around you will put you in the know.

One exercise I have found helpful for heightening awareness of your impact, similar to a 360 but a little riskier, is a facilitated group feedback session. For example, I was leading a sales team and as part of my personal growth, I asked the team to evaluate my performance as a leader. What were the positives and negatives about my leadership over the past six months? I left the meeting room for an hour and asked them to put pluses on one side and minuses on the other, and don't hold back. We did not discuss the results that day.

I asked one of the more trusted and experienced people to debrief me a couple days later after she had collated the results. What was interesting to me was the divergent opinions of my leadership by person (the combined feedback was anonymous but with a small team I could tell who was saying what). It really helped me adjust my approach with some individuals, who were not receiving me the way that I had hoped. With others, I was able to continue as I was with higher confidence because I now knew it was working for them. Through having the courage to get things out on the table, I was able to connect much better with all members of my team. My self-awareness of both my faults and strengths was not high. Even though I knew something felt tense when interacting with certain people, I lacked the specifics on how I was creating tension and, therefore, did not know how to get past it.

People tell you what they think you want to hear, but you really need to probe in a genuine way to understand your true impact. Attempting to establish higher rapport with colleagues to the point that they will feel comfortable sharing whatever concerns they have is worth your time. The reason people are not frank with their bosses is because of safety. They don't want to be reprimanded, fired, or compromise any good standing they have with their boss by showing weakness. This is a sign of lower trust, and they know that the best way to avoid negative consequences is to remain silent about any weakness their own boss may have. Advice to leaders. When one of your team has the courage to be frank with you, thank them and let them know you are learning. Even if you have been in the role a long time, this sort of humility is disarming.

The reality is that bosses determine career trajectory, pay, working conditions, and employment. Until you make the person feel safe and secure enough that they will not be disadvantaged by speaking the truth about your own impact on them and others, you won't hear the truth. In order to do this, you need to be overt about why you want this information (self-awareness/development/build a better workplace, and so on) to put their mind at ease. If necessary, assure them that the information will never be used against them.

When you do hear feedback that is tough, you need to sincerely thank them and even get their advice on how best to improve, which will help build their value and destroy the crazy notion that bosses are all-knowing and perfect. This humility will help establish higher rapport and trust in your working relationship and increase that person's value to you and the team. Feeling valued at work is strongly correlated with commitment and discretionary effort. Self-awareness with the help of your trusted team is a critical step for a high functioning team!

Conclusion

Being the Best Boss Ever requires a high level of conviction as described in section 1. Having a clear *vision*, *following through* on your commitments, valuing *clarity*, being *persistent*, and gaining *confidence* are all qualities that great frontline leaders exude.

Section 2 describes how important being a source of Inspiration is for frontline leaders. In order to be inspiring for individuals, frontline leaders need to turn their focus toward supporting their team members. This involves the ability to *listen*, being *curious* about concerns and ambitions of their valued team members, having *empathy* for and *belief* in others, and being an enlightened *coach* that is helpful instead of threatening.

If you ask any employee to list key attributes of great leaders, they will place "lead by example" at or near the top of the list. Section 3 highlights some components of leading by example that great frontline leaders do: treat people fairly, be honest, reserve judgement, have integrity, and be self-aware.

Of course, all three sections and fifteen chapters are intended to work together, and through review, practice, and making mistakes, become embedded in the muscle memory of great frontline leaders. As you reflect on how well you measure up to each of the topics presented in this book, a cautionary note: don't aim for immediate mastery of all subjects. This will be onerous, depressing, and likely unsustainable.

Instead, my recommendation is select one area that you believe is vital in your organization and that you know you are falling short on. This is likely and area where you do not possess an innate aptitude. Spend time getting better, reading, and getting feedback from trusted colleagues.

Gradually, you will turn an area that is a deficit into a reasonable skill and with persistence maybe even a strength.

In addition, I would advise focusing personal development time on one of the fifteen areas (chapters) where it comes easy to you. Developing this area of strength can be motivational and rewarding. Becoming exceptional in one or more leadership areas increases your confidence and flows over to other leadership qualities. You can also be a mentor for other colleagues struggling in an area you find easy. Perhaps they can reciprocate with one of your deficit areas of a trusted colleague and together you will get stronger.

Becoming a great frontline leader is both daunting and straightforward. If you start with an open mind and allow yourself to be influenced by all of the good leadership examples and advice, the sky is the limit. Understanding critical leadership concepts is the easy part. Adopting practices in line with those concepts is the difficult part. As mentioned above, starting with a commitment to a couple of development areas is an easy way to make progress in the right direction. When those skills become embedded (be sure to confirm that with those around you), then it makes sense to pick some additional leadership skills to improve.

Given what I have witnessed in front line leaders, finding time for learning and improving is the most difficult barrier. As highlighted in chapter 1 (Vision), make time for improvement, such as developing yourself needs to be a proactive pursuit. Nobody is going to give you time for personal development, so you are going have to prioritize it yourself. Put an "unavailable" appointment in the calendar in advance and don't let the crisis of the moment distract you from this critical focus. The more you do this and get proactive with yourself and your business, the more you and your team will rise above crisis mode and thrive.

Good luck on your journey and congratulations on challenging yourself in one of the most difficult and rewarding pursuits possible: being the Best Boss Ever!

Acknowledgements

I am very grateful for having advance input on the keys to successful front-line leadership from twelve highly successful leaders in their field who are all extremely busy and were kind enough to share their wisdom. They are Ian McIver, Dan O'day, Dave Oldreive, Dr. Mike Negraeff, Andrew Thorne, Geoff Brick, Ken Seitz, Bruce Luxmoore, Michelle Newton, Jim Rogers, Karl Pierzchajlo, and Dave Newton.

I would like to thank Mike Skrypnek for providing the spark and early advice for writing a book. To my long-trusted colleague Catherine Hawkins, thank you for always encouraging me to share my views on leadership more and for keeping me on task over the years. To my brother, Brian Dorey, who took a chance on me as a budding leadership coach twenty years ago, taught me all I know about leadership and provided the right support and encouragement to make leadership advice my career. I would like to thank my wonderful wife, Robyn Pickering, for her patience, support, and advice to keep on plodding with this book writing adventure.

Finally, a big thank you to Friesen Publishing for their guidance, advice, and patience.

www.ingramcontent.com/pod-product-compliance
Lightning Source LLC
Chambersburg PA
CBHW040952170526
45159CB00013B/3113